JUMP

LARRY MILLER

CHAIRMAN OF THE JORDAN BRAND

& LAILA LACY

JUMP

MY SECRET JOURNEY FROM THE STREETS TO THE BOARDROOM

WM

WILLIAM MORROW
An Imprint of HarperCollins*Publishers*

HarperCollins books may be purchased for educational, business, or sales promotional use. For information, please email the Special Markets Department at SPsales@harper collins.com

FIRST EDITION

Designed by Elina Cohen

Library of Congress Cataloging-in-Publication Data has been applied for.

ISBN 978-0-06-299981-8

22 23 24 25 26   FRI   10 9 8 7 6 5 4 3 2 1

LAILA LACY

This book is dedicated to the divine ancestors who protect and guide us on our path, to my beloved husband, Jason, and to my children, my immortality, Asali, Ananda, and Jason, Jr.

LARRY MILLER

I dedicate this book to Catherine and Lonnie Miller, Grandmom Mattie, Uncle Roy, and all those who saw something in me when I didn't see it in myself.

CONTENTS

CONTENTS

JUMP

INTRODUCTION

*N*iketown in L.A. was lit up that Saturday in 1999 when we unveiled Air Jordan 15.

It was my unveiling as well, coming out in public as the first president of Jordan Brand, a new sports apparel division of Nike. We weren't just rolling out a new sneaker named after the most famous basketball player of all time; we were introducing a new shoe just when Michael Jordan was retiring from the court. Could Air Jordans still take off if the man who made them fly was off the court?

"You can pull it off," Phil Knight told me when he plucked me from head of Nike's U.S. Apparel to run the new Jordan Brand. But there were plenty of doubters.

We had built the launch around Stevie Wonder's song "Overjoyed," a melodic love ballad that left listeners feeling uplifted and blissful. The song backed up a commercial that included images of Ray Allen, Eddie Jones, Randy Moss, Derek Jeter, and Roy Jones Jr. After the cameos, the camera focused on Michael Jordan, dressed in casual clothes, and gradually pulled away, leaving the viewer with a sense that MJ was still the force behind the sports scene, even as he was yielding his role to the next generation of champions.

We needed to use "Overjoyed" to make the commercial work. Stevie was doubtful at first. I got him on the phone.

"If Michael Jordan called me and asked me," he said, "I'd do it."

Michael called Stevie, and Stevie was in.

But we decided it would be better to have Mary J. Blige sing Stevie's song in the actual commercial. She has a beautiful voice and was more with the current scene. Same deal: She wanted to hear from MJ. He called her, and then he called me.

"Hey, man," he said, "I called Mary. I had to talk to everybody in the damn neighborhood. The person who answered said: 'Yo! Yo, Michael Jordan's on the phone!' I'm talking to Aunt Suzy and Cousin Joe. I'm on the phone a half hour before I get to Mary. She's good with it."

The whole town seemed to be there the night of the launch. Snoop Dogg showed up with Ice Cube. Phil Knight and the whole Nike leadership team was there. MJ, of course. The place was humming. At first Stevie Wonder said he wasn't coming, until his teenage son heard MJ would be there. Great, I'm thinking. Mary Blige, not so much.

"Oh, man, Stevie's here," she said to me backstage. "I don't know if I can do this in front of Stevie."

Thirty minutes later her deep, soulful voice filled the hall. The room went quiet, then thundered with applause. MJ took the stage.

In the back of the room, I exhaled, perhaps for the first time since I had walked into the place. I took a sip of ginger ale, leaned back, and closed my eyes. Just then I felt a tap on my shoulder and clenched up. I sucked in my breath. Was this the tap on the shoulder I had been dreading for the past two decades? A cop? A judge? A lawyer?

It was Phil Knight. He wrapped me up in a hug, shook my hand, and walked into the chaos.

I looked around at the room and wondered: How the hell did I get here? No one in the room knew the real Larry Miller. The man who, at the age of sixteen, shot another teen in a gang tragedy. The man who had been convicted of a series of armed robberies at the age of twenty-five. I thought back twenty years ago to my cell inside Pennsylvania's Graterford State Penitentiary, where I had been serving a sentence for armed robbery. I thought back to a pivotal job interview just before my graduation from Temple University in 1982. Fresh out of prison, armed with top grades and strong recommendations, I was launching my career in accounting. Job offers were rolling in, but there was one I really wanted—Arthur Andersen, one of the Big Eight accounting firms in Philadelphia, my hometown. I had put on my one-and-only suit and tie for a job interview with their lead recruiting partner. I was certain that I was about to land my first full-time gig with a major accounting firm. I was thirty-two and graduating with honors. I was confident that I could handle the work, but I was nervous.

"Why us?" the recruiting executive asked. "I'm sure you've had plenty of offers."

He was right. Top companies like Arthur Andersen were taking heat for their all-white rosters. I was Black and qualified, and I had received offers from at least five other firms. But the Andersen brand was strong. It was on top, and that was where I wanted to be.

We sat in his office. He took his jacket off. I kept mine on. I could feel beads of sweat running down my back.

"You know I have interviewed with a number of your partners," I said. He nodded. I had completed an exhaustive prospective-employee questionnaire and interviewed up the line. "I feel very comfortable with them and the overall welcoming environment of your firm."

But I didn't feel comfortable in my own skin. Yeah, I would have that degree from Temple, but not the "regular" way. I had completed the degree while I was on education release from Graterford State Penitentiary. I had just completed a four-year and nine-month sentence for armed robbery. The self-assured, aspiring accountant in the modest suit was a felon still living in a halfway house.

Should I come clean? I was well aware of the risk of unburdening myself to the executive in a public accounting firm, but all signs indicated I was on the path to landing my first big job.

"Look," I said. "I have something to tell you that did not come out in the applications or the interviews."

He leaned forward, listening intently.

I rolled out the armed robberies, my time behind bars, the community-college courses in which I excelled and the Temple classes I took while living in a halfway house. I did not mention the homicide.

"You know I really like everything you are as a company," I said. "And I know it would be a good fit for both of us."

I watched his face fall. I kept going.

"And I really believe I can make my home here and be a great asset to your company. I wanted to be straight with you and start off with a clean slate."

He forced a smile.

"Wow—that's quite a story," he said. "I am so proud of you for what you've been able to accomplish. I so appreciate the fact that you shared this with me."

He paused. My heart pounded. It was the only sound in the room.

He turned back and reached into his jacket. Sweat trickled down my spine. I thought I was home free.

"I have an offer letter here to give you," he said. "But I can't do it. I can't take a chance on one of our clients coming back to me with this if something were to happen down the line."

I was crushed.

"I get it," I said. I breathed deep and shivered.

We both stood up and shook hands. He put on his jacket, walked me out of his office, and said: "Good luck. You'll do fine."

AND I WOULD.

But I would never ever reveal my prison past to anyone again. Not to friends or coworkers. Never to bosses. No one outside of my close family and my prison buddies knew. Nobody talked. The secret was born. It has lived within me for more than three decades, corroding me from the inside, haunting me day and night, bringing me to my knees with migraine headaches and awful dreams.

The nightmares would sometimes begin with my getting busted for something, or me on my way to jail, or sometimes with me in a jail or some kind of holding cell. Or I would be working, or at home, in some familiar space and living this extraordinary life that I've built. Suddenly I'd be arrested for something vague and tossed back behind bars, losing it all. The circumstances were always cloudy. Something's happened, or maybe I had some years to finish up from a prior sentence. I'm trying to work it out, fix things so I can get back to my life. My motivation throughout the dream is usually to get the issue resolved quickly so I can get to work on time, make a meeting, or keep an appointment.

"You don't understand" was my constant refrain. "I'm not supposed to be here. Let me out!"

I would wake up in a cold sweat.

In real life I could be at a media event to roll out a new sneaker. I'd get a tap on the shoulder. I turn around wondering if the person will say, "Are you the Larry Miller who went to jail for doing stickups in Philly?"

Busted.

Every few months I would have that dream. Over and over.

As I rose through the ranks in business—from Campbell Soup Company to Jantzen, from Jordan Brand to the Portland

Trail Blazers and back—the stakes got higher and the night-mares more debilitating.

The nightmares never allowed me to forget the past I carried with me every single day. But that past life also armed me. It helped me retain the fortitude of the streets, to put on the hard shell we wore to survive in the penitentiary. Prison life forced me to build a barrier and wall off my emotions. If you showed fear or anxiety, that was seen as a sign of weakness, and weak-nesses were exploited. Even if you were having those vulnerable thoughts or feelings, you could never show them.

Those barriers have carried over to a certain degree to how I am today—for better or worse—even in the business world. Show weakness and invite failure. How fearful can I be at a board meeting over whether a deal might fall through when I have put a gun to the head of a drug dealer because I thought he might have shorted me? Why would I show a lack of firmness across the table from a competitor when I have seen an inmate kill a prison guard for denying seconds? My reputation on the streets was "thorough," as in "Larry Miller will follow through and get things done"—take care of business, so to speak—even if that meant extortion. In the business world that has given me the air of a man of mystery, even-keeled, impenetrable—almost like a ghost.

The nightmares and remoteness were prices I had to pay for carrying this secret around for so long. I have walked and lived, day after day, in a world that didn't know anything about my past. I was split in two.

Up on that stage at Niketown, Michael Jordan interrupted

my contemplation. I took another deep breath. I understood and accepted the fact that the people who stood around me sipping champagne and appreciating MJ probably assumed that I had started my life and career more or less as they had. Went to school, learned a lot, worked hard, and pulled myself up to the top of my game. While that story is true, it's also incomplete.

No one knew that my view from the top included so much of the bottom, where I started. Not my friends, not my neighbors, and definitely not my colleagues.

The secret will die because of this book.

I

THE CHAMP

*T*he first time a cop stuck a gun in my face, I was twelve years old.

My friend Tyrone Mayo and I were heavy into bikes back then—breaking them down, fixing them up, and cruising West Philly's narrow streets. One summer afternoon we were biking up to Pep Boys on Market Street to get some parts. Tyrone was sitting on the crossbar. We were riding up Hazel Avenue, and we saw this brand-new, red English Racer parked outside a row house. We were both like, "Damn!"

"Man," Tyrone said, "if that bike's there when we come back, I'm taking it."

Tyrone and I went on to Pep Boys, did whatever we were doing, and when we came back, the bike was still there. "Man," he said, "let me off." He jumped on the English Racer, and we took off.

We brought the bike back to his house. We were in the

backyard stripping the bike down, joking and laughing. Out of nowhere, a man and a woman came walking up to us and one of them said: "Can I see that bike please?" Tyrone and I looked at each other, terrified—like *Oh, shit!*

I took off running through the house. Just as I made it out the front door, a cop waiting there pulled his gun.

"Stop," he said, "or I'll blow your brains out!"

We were arrested, and I ended up getting sentenced to probation.

LOOKING BACK ON my early days in West Philly, I guess I was lucky to have come away in one piece. Lucky to have stayed out of reform school or jail for even longer. Lucky to have avoided being shot or beaten to a pulp in the gang wars that were a regular fact of life.

There was the time my cousin rescued me from a bully when I was barely five.

And the time I left the fresh vegetable stand where I was working to get a hoagie just as a rival gang showed up to get revenge on me for beating down of one of their members.

I even had a run-in with Juanita Kidd Stout, the first African-American woman to serve as a judge in Pennsylvania. She was ready to throw me in jail when a stroke of luck saved me.

Luck and my family—a crazy, loving, laughing, brawling cast of characters. Role models, good and bad, but a steady sense of love and support.

One of the significant things about our family while I was

growing up was that, unlike some families in the neighborhood, we always encouraged one another. From the time I could remember, my uncle Roy used say, "That boy right there, he's a champ." Roy came back from the Korean War with a messed-up head, but in his lucid moments he used to talk about my becoming a lawyer or some other type of professional. He helped instill in me the belief that I could be whatever I wanted to be. Mom, my father, Lon—everybody—were always very supportive of that idea. I was lucky to have that sense of wholeness you get from a strong family.

EVEN BEFORE I reached my teens, I became good at making trouble. I wasn't the biggest kid around. I was on the small and wiry side, but I was smart and knew how to fight at an early age.

I was eight years old when my younger sister, Gloria, burst through the front door crying. "That boy slapped me in the face," she said.

I had fists and an anger management problem before I hit double digits. I walked down the block, found the kid in question. "You like to slap little girls?" I asked. I beat his ass, and I did it in front of his friends to make sure they all got the message. No one would mess with any one of my four sisters without paying a price.

The West Philly I came up in during the 1950s and '60s was a sixty-block concentration of poor and working-class, largely African-American families, living in small row houses between the Schuylkill River and Cobbs Creek Park. Market Street divides Philly by the north and south. It cuts right through City Hall, where William Penn stands over the so-called City of Brotherly Love. But by the time it reached our neighborhood sixty streets uptown, it was a teeming hub of buses and subway lines with vegetable markets, shoe stores, corner groceries, and beauty parlors.

My parents and their families came up to Philly from North Carolina during the Great Migration in the 1940s.

Lonnie was the first of the two to come to Philly. His father, Garland Miller, was a farmer in Rutherfordton, North Carolina, a tiny town between Charlotte and Asheville. He married Lon's mother, Hattie Forney.

My mother, Catherine, also grew up in the Jim Crow era in the tiny town of Statesville, North Carolina. Her mother, Mattie, and her five brothers went north first and left Catherine with her ailing father. She had a sister who had already passed away. Catherine's father, Walter Samuel Jones, had worked in the tobacco fields. Walter fell ill, and Catherine stayed with him down south until he died, then came up to Philadelphia to join Mattie and her five brothers. She arrived in her teens and graduated from West Philadelphia High School.

It was a similar situation with Lon. My aunt Vi, who was his oldest sister, moved up to Philly. Then all the other brothers and sisters followed. Catherine moved in with her mother on the same block as Lon. They met and married in the early 1940s and started to have kids, many kids, one after another, eight altogether. Our first house was on Fifty-Seventh and Ludlow Streets.

Lonnie was a quiet, hardworking man. For most of our lives he did shift work at U.S. Gypsum, a factory that made drywall. The plant ran 24-7, and Lon would leave early for the 8 A.M. to 4 P.M. shift, sometimes the 4 P.M. to midnight, or the all-night shift from midnight to 8 A.M. I can't say that we kids were all that respectful of his need for rest, but he would rarely get angry with us. The most he would say was "Stop all that noise," especially when he was watching baseball.

Lon loved to watch the major leagues. He loved the Athletics, then the Phillies. Matter of fact, he named me Larry after his favorite player, Larry Doby, the second Black player in the major leagues and the first in the American League.

Lon had style. On a Saturday night, he would dress to the nines: gray flannel suit, overcoat with wide lapels, a Camel no-filter hanging out of his mouth, always a Camel. Weekends were Lon's time to party and drink, sometimes too much.

WITH LONNIE WORKING shifts at the plant and watching baseball in the living room, Catherine ran the household.

Mom ruled with southern charm and northern ferocity. She didn't take any crap off anybody. She had to be that way. She was tall and thin with warm brown skin and kind eyes, full of love and laughter, but she did not play, and we all knew it. She had eight kids there, plus Grandmom Mattie, and a bunch of other folks around the house all the time, including Uncle Roy.

The Army had given Uncle Roy a 100 percent disability rating after the Korean War, but there was nothing wrong with him, physically. He had what we now call severe post-traumatic stress disorder. He went off the deep end at times.

There was a time we were all eating around the table, about ten of us. We were laughing and talking. The table was piled high with food and plates. Uncle Roy got upset with something in the conversation, left the table, and came back with an ax.

"I'm tired of this shit," he said. He swung the ax over his head and chopped the table in half.

Some nights he would wake up and roam around until morning. One night he'd come down in the wee hours, turned over everything on the first floor, and flung chairs against the wall. Mom was furious, but cool. We kids looked around amazed for a minute. Then we started to put it all back.

"No!" Mom said. "Y'all leave it just like that. He turned that shit over—he gon' fix it." She looked at Roy, who was twice her size, walked over, and stared up into his face as he begged her not to put him out. "You can stay. I'm not gon' put you out. But you gotta take your crazy somewhere else."

As crazy as it was—and it got really crazy at times—it was always family first. We hung together, we took care of one another as best we could, we looked out for each other in the house and on the streets.

"We may not have much," Lon would say, "but we do have each other."

MOM FELT THE same but had a pointed way of showing it.

Uncle Roy and his buddies would hang out in and around the

house, smoking and drinking rotgut wine. Wild Irish Rose was top-shelf for them. They called themselves "the good men."

"All of y'all together don't make one good man," she would say and laugh and shoo them off the front steps.

What I didn't appreciate at the time was the discrimination these strong men faced. They had put their lives on the line on the battlefields of World War II and Korea and returned to a country that not only didn't value their service but refused to even acknowledge their basic rights as American citizens. They still faced job and housing discrimination, voter disenfranchisement, unequal protection under the law.

Mom also understood the bottom line: The family had used Uncle Roy's VA loan to buy the house we were all living in. Uncle Roy stayed. But after he busted up the table, Mom gathered us kids, took us down to the drugstore at the corner, got on the pay phone, and started to look for a new home. We were in Uncle Roy's house, and it was time for us to find our own.

Mom and Lonnie pulled together their savings and bought a small row house on Catharine Street, between the Cobbs Creek and Cedar Park neighborhoods. Eight of us shared one bathroom. When we moved in, a white family was moving out next door. More on that later.

We had a blast on Catharine Street. My oldest brother, Bill, was in the Air Force; Jerry eventually joined the Army. Ted was still very young. It was party time when they came home from Vietnam. My sisters, Leon, Glo, Theresa, and Flo, would put on talent shows, like Lawrence Welk had come to West Philly. We were coming up in a strong community where everyone worked hard.

Men and women had decent blue-collar jobs. Schools were nearby, and we walked home from school for lunch.

We made it work.

I WAS A good kid back then. I earned my title "the Champ."

All through elementary school, I was the teacher's pet, a straight-A student, always the smartest kid in the class. Grandmom Mattie even framed one of my straight-A report cards and hung it on the wall. Like many families in those days before the internet, we had a *Britannica Junior Encyclopedia* set on the bookshelf. That's where I learned about everything from Antarctica and aardvarks down to xylophones and zeppelins.

My elementary school teachers looked at me as a kid they could trust. They made me the "Outside Messenger." They would give me bus passes and send me to stores for supplies, or to deliver messages from one school to another, or to pick up stuff from downtown and bring it back.

"Larry's in charge," Catherine would tell my brothers and sisters when she left the house to run errands.

When I was as young as ten, Mom even trusted me to take my little brothers and sisters to Center City Philadelphia to events like the Mummers Parade on New Year's Day and the Thanksgiving Day Parade. They were the two times every year when everyone from Philly and the suburbs—Black or white, rich or not—would show up downtown to see the wild Mummers strut down Broad Street on New Year's or the marching bands and floats of Thanksgiving. Downtown Philly was a madhouse.

"Now y'all listen to Larry," she would tell my siblings.

And I would navigate us through the city on public transportation.

It would be me; Leen (Eileen), who was a year younger than me; Glo (Gloria), who was a year younger than Leen; my brother Ted, who was a year younger than Glo; and sometimes Flo (Florence), who was a couple years younger than Ted. Theresa was a baby and too young to go. The others were as young as five, six, and seven. We would walk over to Market Street, hand in hand. We would catch the El, the elevated subway line, and then walk it from there. They were too scared not to listen to me. They all knew they'd get lost and never make it home without me.

We would go all the way downtown, watch the parade, and then come back home. It meant so much that Mom believed that I was responsible enough to handle getting everybody there and back safely. And there weren't any cell phones or anything like that we could use to check in. We were on our own all the way there, and all the way home.

To this day, I feel a sense of responsibility for all of my brothers and sisters. That was my job. That was part of my role. I still feel like I'm supposed to take care of everybody, even though I'm not the oldest of the family, and it all started with herding all the little ones to the Mummers Parade and back.

I COULD BE trusted to fight if I had to.

We had a cousin on Mom's side of the family named Walt who lived with us for a time. I was around five years old, and I used to hang out with a kid named Jackie, another named Warren, and a few others. They were all older and a little bigger and would do mean-kid stuff like beat up on the smaller kids. One time they were picking on me, and Cousin Walt came up the street. He saw my face all upset and asked me what was wrong. When I told him, the boys started to run away. Walt grabbed Jackie and Warren, told me to get a stick, and said, "Now get 'em!"

I beat the hell out of those boys with that stick. They had been bothering me and being mean, so Walt just held them for what felt like forever. I went to work on both of them, but I think Jackie got the worst of it. He was crying and I was going to town on him.

I ran into Jackie many years later when I was a teenager in the Cedar Avenue gang. He was from another gang called the Barbary Coast, but we weren't fighting each other at the time. We talked for a few minutes and got caught up really quick.

Jackie got shot dead shortly after that.

I LOOKED UP to my oldest brother, Billy, a lot, too, but he went off to the Vietnam War, so he wasn't around much. Then my brother Jerry returned from the war and became more of a role model to me, but Jerry was crazy.

Back when we were all very little, Mom would leave him in charge, and he would drive everybody insane. He wore us out! Nobody could tease you like Jerry. He would come in the house, and we would just try to be quiet because nobody wanted to draw his attention and be his first victim. Then he would just randomly pick somebody out and it was their day, and Jerry would ride you until you cried. He would tease us to the point where we would want to kill him.

One day Jerry was babysitting all of us, and I was reading a book. I loved to read. I could devour two books a week. Anyway, Jerry narrowed his eyes at me, and even though I wasn't looking at him, I could feel his stare.

"Hey, smarty-pants," he said. "You gon' get straight As again this year? You still the teacher's pet? I'd like to pet your teacher."

Eventually I had had enough. I grabbed a knife from the kitchen and ran after him. He ran into the bathroom and locked the door. He sat inside the bathroom, and I stayed outside the door yelling, "I'm gonna kill you!"

Then I pretended to walk away from the door, making loud footsteps, hoping that he would open it to check.

Ted was watching and he yelled, "He's still here, Jerry!"

I screamed at Ted, "I'll kill you, too!"

Like I said, I had some anger issues at an early age. I was cool and calm—until I wasn't.

I ALWAYS HAD a little hustle going, even when I was in elementary school. Shoveling snow, or whatever I could find to make cash. We lived next door to an old white lady. One winter when I was about seven or eight, we got hit with a lot of snow and I worked my ass off shoveling the front of her house. When I finished cleaning it all up, she paid me a nickel. I went inside the house, sat down, and cried. I couldn't believe she gave me a nickel, as hard as I had worked. I was little, but I was learning about the value of my time.

I took a step up with my very first job, which was selling *Jet* and *Ebony* magazines door-to-door. I was maybe nine or ten. There was a guy who lived across the street from us who was like a distributor. I would go over and get my supply of *Jet* every week. I made a nickel and he got a dime for every sale. *Ebony* was a monthly and went for like thirty-five cents each, and I made fifteen cents off each sale of those. I was always willing to hustle and make a little money.

WHEN WE MOVED to the smaller house on Catharine Street, we discovered the true meaning of a family making it in tight quarters. However, living in the "working class," we felt rich. It was truly the village that took care of everyone.

Grandmom had moved in with a friend in an apartment on Race Street all the way across town on the north side of Market Street, but I used to walk over and see her all the time.

Bill Withers's song "Grandma's Hands" always reminds me of her to this day. I picture her hands holding mine, or her clapping in church when she used to take me with her. Withers talked about how walking with his grandma on her shopping trips was "the best job in the world." I felt the same way. I used to walk with Grandmom so she could do her shopping and buy whatever she needed, which was generally not much.

"Grandmom," I would ask her, "can I get this candy?"—or whatever. She would keep her money tied up in a handkerchief.

She would open up her little handkerchief and take out her coins and dollar bills. She would give me a few cents to come along with her, more of a reward than a payday, but she knew she didn't have to. That was my job, and I was proud to be by her side.

I always just kinda knew that I was her favorite, and she and I always hung out. She passed away on New Year's Day, 1963. Sad times for the whole family, especially me.

IN SCHOOL THE teachers would appoint crossing guards and safety patrols to make sure little students could cross the streets without getting run over. I liked the fact that kids on the team could wear sashes across their chests with badges. I always liked uniforms and that kind of stuff as a kid. So, I volunteered to be a "safety," put on the badge before school and again when it let out. By sixth grade I had worked my way up to a captain's badge.

I was guiding kids across Cedar Avenue in front of Bryant Elementary School one afternoon when a few middle school kids strolled by.

"Hey, look at Captain Larry," one of them said. I had my arms raised up and out because cars were rushing by, but they pushed on through and crossed the street, right in front of traffic. One kid looked back at me. "Gonna arrest us, Captain Larry?"

That was the start of my questioning my cool. Did I really want to be the good boy who got the best grades, pleased the adults, and earned their trust?

The question became more persistent in the early 1960s when West Philly started to change. We found ourselves on the front lines of integration when we were bused to unwelcoming schools. White families moved out if they could, and much of the city government's investment went with them. Over time the city quit cleaning the streets or picking up the garbage as often. What had been a village where families looked out for one another slowly began to lose its sense of order and community. The white folks who stayed were pissed off. Police cruisers rode in front of the school bus to fend off white kids who threw bricks at the windows while our little brown heads ducked in fear. All those changes heightened our anxiety and shredded the insulation of our village.

The neighborhood shifted from tight-knit self-sufficiency into survival mode. And so did I.

2

HOMICIDE

One summer day in 1965 when I was sixteen, my buddies and I were playing ball at Sherwood Playground on Fifty-Sixth and Christian Streets when my girlfriend, Karen, showed up. She was trouble and looked it with her pressed hair, halter top, tight jeans, and high-heel platforms. She got into more beefs than anyone. She sashayed onto the court and said, "We gotta talk."

We walked around the corner. She pulled out a pistol.

"I got this gun," she said, "and I want you to hold it for me."

She held up a silver, nine millimeter semi-automatic, finger on the trigger, business end to the sky. She cocked her head and smiled.

"What are you doing with this?" I asked.

Karen thought she was a gangster. She had gotten into it with one of the older guys from around the way. We called them "old heads." They'd had words, and she wouldn't back down. I had to step in and work it out. When it was all over, me and the old head wound up drinking wine and laughing it off.

Karen got off on picking fights and talking shit to everyone. I always found myself jumping between her and my buddies just to keep her from getting beat up.

"I'm going to shoot his ass. Just hold this for me."

She put the cold, silver gun in my hand. It felt weighty, almost like it was wired to a source of power. I wrapped my hand around the grip, slipped my finger over the trigger, and touched it lightly, very lightly.

"I'll keep it for you," I said.

BY THE MID-1960S, gangs and crews had carved our West Philly neighborhood into private territories, block by block. We found power in controlling everything, from who walked down the street, to who got to date certain girls, to who was able to shop in certain stores. We organized ourselves into tiny kingdoms, often controlled by teenagers who answered to old heads. Gangs, not police, enforced our own style of law and order.

In the ten square miles where we grew up, a bunch of gangs fought for control of the streets: the Creek, the Moon, Woodland Avenue, Barbary Coast, Pine Street. There were some others.

I had graduated elementary school at the top of my class, still "the Champ," still feeling fine about being the trusted, smart kid. But sometime around sixth or seventh grade, the streets became more important to me. It was a shift. Not quite a radical change. More of an embrace of the violence that happened around us, that was part of our daily lives.

By the time I entered junior high school, I had left the good boy behind.

At the very beginning of one summer in my early teens, I was sitting on the steps one night with a guy named Carl Young. We were drinking cheap wine from a pint bottle and smoking Newports.

"You know what, Carl? This summer I'm gonna get me a rep."

There was no single thing that made me flip. It might have been that cop shoving a pistol in my face and threatening to blow my brains out. It might have been raw ambition. Maybe my brother Jerry and his wild friends rubbed off on me. I came to realize power was on the street, not in the classroom. People who stood out, who made a mark, were street hustlers. If you wanted to make a rep for yourself in those days, if you wanted to become a leader—someone respected and feared—you joined a gang.

I flipped from being the straight-A student, on the right track, and jumped on the track to becoming a grade A gangster. I didn't care what the teachers thought anymore. I wanted to be known as "that dude" in the street. Being a good student and all of that just wasn't cool anymore.

I was drawn, slowly but surely, to the Cedar Avenue gang. It made geographic sense. Cedar Avenue was a residential strip with a few bars, grocery stores, and churches sprinkled about, a block north of our new row house on Catharine Street. Plus, my buddies up and down the street were in with Cedar Avenue. It felt right.

IT OBVIOUSLY FELT wrong to my parents. Catherine cornered me many times on our small front porch and asked me whether I had done my homework. I might not even have gone to school that day. I talked my way back out of the house and onto the streets.

"Show me your homework," she would demand. "I want to see it now!"

"Aw, Mom," I would tell her, "I finished it at school and left it in my locker."

On some occasions, that might have been true.

Lon was not in the best position to steer me away from gang life. Working shifts at U.S. Gypsum kept him away from the neighborhood. One time on the way home after work he saw me on the corner with my buddies, a cigarette hanging from the corner of my mouth.

Lon pulled over, got out of his car, yanked a handkerchief from his pocket, took a drag from his Camel, and blew it through the white cloth. The smoke turned it a hazy shade of tan.

"See what this is doing to your lungs?" he asked. He shoved it in my face. "Why would you want to do that to yourself?"

The irony of him going through a pack of Camels while asking me to quit smoking was lost on him. Maybe that was why I didn't listen. I loved my old man, but our worlds were separating. Lon and Mom saw my drift from the classroom to the streets. I got the lectures about a good education being the way to success in life and a job that paid well. But I couldn't see past the crowd of kids who gathered every day on the street corners or met in someone's house whose parents were out working. I had done the smart-kid thing; I was looking for something different.

Shortly after we moved and I started middle school, Mom

went to work outside our home. She took a full-time job at Philadelphia International Airport. The woman who had run the household now worked the four-to-twelve shift cleaning restrooms. Over time, she got promotion after promotion and retired as a manager. She appreciated her independence and started to enjoy more of her life.

And so did I.

With Lon and Mom out of the house most of the day, and my days in public school practically over, I built a life on the streets. I was solidifying my reputation for being a "thorough" dude. If anyone crossed me, they suffered the consequences. Even in that disorganized and violent world, my word meant something.

All of this meant more time spent at reform school, more officially the Youth Study Center, as in the juvenile detention center, incarceration for kids like me. I got out of the Youth Study Center right after school started in 1964. I began attending John Bartram High School, sometimes. Then I got arrested again for something minor; I don't even remember what it was. This time I had to go before Judge Juanita Kidd Stout, the first Black woman to serve as a judge in Pennsylvania. She was notorious for being strict and tough.

In the gang, we used to wear our hair processed in these slicked-back hairdos. Judge Stout glided into her courtroom, took her seat, looked us over, and narrowed her eyes. "I want all of you to get your hair cut," she said. "If I see you back in here in front of me again, and you have that mess in your hair, I'm sending you to jail."

So, we all pretended we would get our hair cut, but we didn't.

We were still wearing our processed 'dos around the neighborhood with pride. One night, we were all out doing what we did. Somehow, I came upon a gun from who knows where. It was a .38 revolver. Me and Monny, my boy from the Cedar Avenue gang, decided to go looking for some of the guys from the Coast, since we had heard there was a party up on some street close by. We were walking up there because, hey, I'm gonna go shoot one of these jokers, right?

We walked up to the house, and there was no party. If there had been a party, it was already over and the house was empty. I kicked the door in, went in, and nobody was in there. Me and Monny were walking back and a cop pulled up right beside us. I tossed the gun into some bushes, but he saw me do it. He jumped out, grabbed me, jammed me up, went over to the bushes, and found the gun. He looked over at Monny and said, "Is he with you?"

I said, "Naw, he ain't with me," and they let him go.

They locked me up, and then I went before a hearing judge, a magistrate. He looked through my records and was just about to release me on my own recognizance until the time for me to go to court. I was telling him that I didn't have the gun and whatever, denying it all. The judge decided to let my parents sign for me to go, but then he looked in the records and said, "Wait a minute . . . didn't Judge Stout tell you to get your hair cut?" She had put it in the official court record.

He said, "I'm going to keep you locked up. I want her to see you with your hair just like that since you didn't get it cut like she told you to."

From there they took me to the Youth Study Center. I kept trying to get a haircut in there, but the magistrate had put on my paperwork that I was not allowed. By now, my hair was looking extra wild and crazy from being locked up for a few days.

This was a Tuesday night, and I was going before Judge Stout on the following Thursday or Friday. I was stressing out because I was sure she was gonna send me to jail. We were all in a lounge-type area playing cards and stuff like that when the phone rang. The counselor who was assigned to us came over and asked me if anybody was home at my house.

I said, "Yeah!"

He said, "Well, there's a chance we might let you out tonight if somebody can come pick you up."

The center had gotten overcrowded, and the authorities had decided to let some people go. Jerry came down, got me out, and brought me home. The next day I went right to the barbershop and got a haircut. A day or two after that I went before Judge Stout. I was denying the gun thing since he didn't find it on me.

"I see you listened to me and got your hair cut," she said.

"Yes, ma'am." It was another stroke of good luck. She was gonna throw the book at my ass.

GUNS WERE STARTING to show up around the neighborhood more and more. The sound of gunfire in the night became common. My friends would occasionally walk up with a pistol in their belt. I had already gone to juvenile detention for a few months just for being in the vicinity when one of my buddies shot a dude we used to call Boney Bill. So, I was no stranger to guns. Nor was I a stranger to getting locked up. It was as if everyone on the block was either going to or coming from jail. It became our normal.

But something about the handgun Karen asked me to hold made me feel, I don't know, invincible.

I showed it to one of my boys named Lamont. He was a big, strong guy. He didn't take shit from anybody. He also knew his way around handguns.

"Man, that's a nice piece!" he said.

"I know," I said. "I ain't giving this back to her."

"How you gonna pull that off?"

I thought about it for a minute. Then I said, "I got it."

Lamont and I walked around the corner. We took the gun to his house and stashed it away. I told him that when we came back into the playground, I wanted him to pretend to be arguing with me. I told him to say something like "Man, you stupid! You shouldn't have done that" and to be really loud about it.

We walked back into the playground and he started going into it. Karen asked what happened, and I told her that some cops rolled by and I had said something to them. Then they chased us and I had to throw the gun to get it off me in case I got caught. I told her not to worry about it, though, because I knew exactly where it was, and we could go right back over there and get it.

"You better find it," she said.

I took her back around the corner and started searching around in some bushes, acting like I was looking for it. Not here. Not there. She stopped me and grabbed me by my shirt.

"You lying muthafucka!" she said. She knew I'd kept it, and she also knew there was nothing she could do about it.

MURDERS WERE ON the rise in Philadelphia, especially in West Philly. Plenty of the shooters were my age, around sixteen. Some were younger, some older, but most were juveniles according to the law. The cops reacted with a vengeance. They were used to smacking us around just for hanging out, but when they heard gunfire, they rolled up in force, asked few questions, rounded everyone up, and saved their interrogations for the precinct house.

Cedar Avenue was at war with the Fifty-Third and Pine gang. Their territory butted right up against ours. A few nights after Karen gave me that pistol to hold, I tucked it into my belt and went out to fight. We got into it with a guy named Erving. I knew him well, but he was with the other gang. He was heating up on one of my guys, so I pulled out the pistol and shot him in the arm. The fight stopped. Everyone ran. By the time we heard sirens we were long gone.

Erving survived. But the hand-to-hand fighting that had been typical in our conflicts did not. Once kids my age started to carry guns, a heightened sense of fear began to permeate the streets. You could feel the violence escalating by the day.

That September a guy from my gang was stabbed and killed. He was a kid who I felt close to and cared about, in part because he was a year or two younger than me. In my head he was still an innocent, a child. His killing really messed me up. I was both sad and enraged.

The last night of September 1965 I was drinking wine with three of my buddies: Monny from our Cedar Avenue gang, Shotgun, and Cheyenne. Shotgun and Chey were from the Sixtieth Street gang, but we were kind of like allies. Plus, they knew the young boy who'd been killed, and they were also looking for revenge.

"C'mon," I said. "Let's find one of those motherfuckers."

I jammed Karen's silver pistol in my waistband.

We left a house on Catharine Street drunk, hit the streets, and headed over to the corner of Fifty-Third and Locust, where we knew the rival gang would be hanging.

"I'm telling you right now," I said. "If we find somebody, I'm going to kill them."

THE CORNER OF Fifty-Third and Locust was halfway between Cedar Avenue and Cobbs Creek.

From a block away, we saw a kid standing on the corner. We approached and circled him.

"Where you from?" I asked.

"Not from around here," he said.

He was about my size, a little taller, maybe a little skinnier. He was immediately outnumbered. He was scared and in no mood to fight. His eyes got wide. He raised his hands in front of his chest, as if to hold us off.

"Yeah you are," I said. "You're with Fifty-Third and Pine. Why else would you be hanging right on this corner?"

"I'm not, I'm not, I'm not with any gang!" he pleaded.

I reached behind, pulled out the gun, pointed it at the kid, squeezed the trigger, and shot him in the chest. He dropped. We turned away and kept on walking.

In my head, that was one down. I was on the hunt for another. That was my mentality. Who's next? We walked five or six blocks deeper into the rival gang's territory.

The shots were still ringing in my ears when we heard sirens. We didn't even have a chance to run when the patrol car pulled up. Before the two cops jumped out, I had enough time to chuck the gun behind some bushes. They didn't see me get rid of it, but they still cuffed us and threw us into a wagon that had rolled up behind the patrol cars.

In hindsight, it was a good thing the police stopped us or we would have kept walking down Locust Street, looking for someone else to shoot. I wasn't even that worried. What did they have on us? No weapon, no witnesses, no evidence.

For all we knew, that kid might have been okay. The gun could have misfired. The bullet might have grazed him. He might have gotten up and walked away.

At least that was what I told myself.

IN THE EIGHTEENTH District station house, the cops split us up and put us into separate interrogation rooms. Two detectives started asking me questions about a shooting a few blocks from where they arrested us.

"I don't know a thing about any shooting," I said. "I was just walking up the street to get a soda."

I thought they were just hassling us with nothing solid. Yeah, I said, we were in the neighborhood and heard some shots, but we didn't see anything or anyone. I stuck to my story. Cheyenne and Shotgun got the same treatment. They stayed cool and didn't admit to anything. I was ready to go. I thought I was so slick and so smart. I even demanded that they give me a lie detector test.

But the cops were working hard on Monny. They told him a kid had been shot dead. If he was connected in any way, if he'd seen it happen or heard the shots or knew of anyone who might have been in on the shooting, he could spend the rest of his life in jail. He was a juvenile but would be prosecuted as an adult.

"You know what happens to cute little boys like you behind bars at night, don't you?" one of the detectives asked.

Monny broke down. He told them I had the gun, that I had confronted a boy and pulled the trigger and all.

By that time, they had found the silver pistol in the bushes, not far from where they had picked us up.

A cop walked into the interrogation room and held the gun a foot from my face: "Hey," he said, "this gun looks like the one used in a homicide tonight."

Homicide. The word floated in the precinct station's stale, smoky air. You mean that boy didn't get up and walk away? We had gone out that night looking for revenge, but I didn't fully understand what that would look like. It was starting to become clearer. I sat back and closed my eyes. I almost cried before I caught myself and regained my defiance.

"I want a lie detector test," I said. Thinking I could beat it, I invented an alternate story. A cop read the results.

"You think you can lie to us and get away with it?" he asked. "Everything you just told us was bullshit."

And my prints were on the gun handle. And Monny had dimed me out. And a boy was dead. I had done unthinkable, irreparable damage, and that reality was setting in.

I didn't get out of the police station that night. I didn't go home for four and a half years.

3

JUVENILE JUSTICE

*T*o this day, I can still hear the loud, deep clang of the medieval metal door closing behind me in Pennsylvania's Eastern State Penitentiary. It was a thick, gigantic, black gate that made these clicking sounds as its gears allowed it to open—then the deafening sound when it slammed shut.

Oh shit! I thought they could never open that door again, not the way that thing slammed shut.

Al Capone and Willie Sutton, the bank robber, had been locked up there. Now it's a tourist site in Philadelphia's Fairmount section as the nation's first true penitentiary. For me it was a stop along the way into four years behind bars.

I HAD JUST turned sixteen, and I was angry—not that I had shot and killed another kid, but that I had gotten caught. By the time I carried that gun into Pine Street gang territory, the streets had made me hard and I had little to no empathy. But the gravity of the situation was now setting in, and with it the remorse that I carry to this day.

With more gang-related homicides all over Philly, and quite a few committed by juveniles like me, the justice system reacted with more severe consequences. Rather than dealing with the root causes of the socioeconomic challenges that drove kids to join gangs and carry guns, judges in juvenile court would waive jurisdiction over cases involving minors, which meant that teenagers could be prosecuted in adult courts. In what I now see as a shortsighted attempt to slow down gang violence, the courts began certifying more and more young people out of the juvenile system. Fourteen-, fifteen-, and sixteen-year-olds were being tried as adults for serious, violent crimes. They went to adult court and did hard time in adult prison.

That was the system I faced.

First stop was the Creek, Philly's juvenile jail, where I was charged but stayed only a few days. From there, I was transferred to Holmesburg Prison, an ancient penitentiary behind massive, fieldstone walls that opened in 1896. It later became notorious for chemical testing on inmates and a prison riot that killed the warden in 1973. Most of the guys in there were adults who were on their way to state or federal prisons. Since I had been in and out of jail from the age of thirteen, it was not an unfamiliar territory or community. There were people I had gotten to know who I never saw on the street, only in jail. When I would go back, they would always be there. It almost felt like a reunion. "Yo! What's up, man?"

THE GUARDS WOKE me up in my cell.

"Hey," one said, "you got visitors."

Lon and Mom were waiting in the visitors' room. They had driven all the way across town to Holmesburg in Philly's far Northeast section. They looked more shaken and shocked than sad. Mom did the talking.

"We're going to do what we can to get you a lawyer," she said, "but looks like you are going to have to live with this. We love you. We are here for you. Everyone misses you."

I was glad to see them, but I was already wearing my tough, prison game face. I had steeled myself to whatever might come my way.

Mom and Lon were devastated that their former "champ" had been arrested for murder. They asked around the community about defense attorneys. They gathered savings, borrowed some money, and put together enough cash to hire a lawyer.

"You got another visitor," a guard told me as he jangled his keys, unlocked my cell, cuffed me, and led me down the cell block.

Abraham Berkowitz—this old, stooped-over, white-haired guy, with scruffy whiskers and yellowed teeth—met me in the common area. We sat across from each other at a table. He was holding a beat-up leather briefcase. He hauled it onto the table, unlatched it, and brought out a stack of what must've been charging documents and affidavits. He looked through some of them. Then he started asking me questions about that night.

"I'm not talking to you," I said.

"What do you mean?" he asked. "Your parents sent me here to help you out."

"Whatever, man," I said. I was dressed in prison blues. They had handcuffed me to the table. "I got nothing to say."

"Look," he said, "I'm not a cop." Berkowitz leaned over and whispered, "You shot and killed someone. Do you want to spend the rest of your life in jail? Go to the electric chair? Do you wanna die? If you keep this up, that's what's going to happen to you. Now, you need to start talking to me. I'm trying to save your life."

That got my attention. I told him what happened that night—how I was drunk, that I thought the kid had walked away, and that I felt awful he had died.

The old lawyer said he would try to get the district attorney to accept a plea deal: seeing that I was, in fact, sixteen, if I would plead guilty to second-degree murder, he would try to keep me in the juvenile system and bargain for reduced jail time.

Berkowitz negotiated what turned out to be a very beneficial deal. I pleaded to second-degree murder and got a sentence of four and a half to twenty years. He also got the court to agree that I could serve most of my time in Camp Hill, which was for inmates up to the age of twenty-one. I would not have to serve time with adult inmates.

Many of the kids my same age who were with me in Holmesburg ended up getting a lot more time, even life sentences for some. If I had gone in and tried to fight it alone without a lawyer, I might still be locked up today.

BUT BEFORE I got to Camp Hill, in the countryside about ten miles south of Harrisburg, I spent three months at Holmesburg in

Philly, and then I had to get through processing at Eastern State Penitentiary.

There was a friend of mine when I was at Holmesburg who was an older cat. He had been through the whole deal. He schooled me on what to expect when I got to Eastern State. He said, "I'm gon' tell you. When you get to Eastern State you gotta watch these old perverted muthafuckas. They'll come at you like 'Oh, I know your family' and all this stuff to try to get your confidence. Then they'll start giving you stuff, and then they'll try you. So, you gotta watch out for that shit."

The first day I got to Eastern State I met up with a friend of mine named Teen, also a young dude, maybe seventeen. He was in the cell right across from mine. We had both just been sentenced and were sent down there to Eastern State. We knew we weren't going to be there very long. And since we were young, they put us in twenty-four-hour lockdown for our protection, away from the general population.

I was in my cell when a guy comes up to the bars. "Yo, uh, is your name Miller?" he asked. "Your name's Larry Miller?"

I said, "Yeah."

"Your father named Lonnie?"

Now, I was worried. "Man, get the fuck away from my cell!"

"Naw, naw. I'm dead serious. Your father named Lonnie? Your mother named Catherine?"

I said, "Who the fuck *are* you? Get away from my cell."

"I'm your cousin, man. Wait, I'll be right back."

He came back with pictures of my whole family. He was my cousin on my dad's side! His name was George. My aunt Helen had like ten or eleven kids, and they all grew up in South Philly. We knew our cousin Sonny because he used to come by the house all the time. I also knew a cousin who we used to call Hershey and another named Junior. I had heard George's name but I never met him before, since he had been in jail for like twenty years. The pictures were of Lon and Mom, and me! He had baby pictures of me up in there. Over the years his mom and the family had sent him pictures of everybody.

We started talking. He had been there so long that by now he had some pull in the jail.

"I'm gonna get you outta here," he said, "in one piece."

They used to ship inmates out to their destinations every Wednesday morning. My buddy Teen had come in late on Wednesday, and I had come in on the following Friday. George said he was going to make sure they got me out of there and up to Camp Hill on next Wednesday's bus.

"What about my boy? Can you help him out, too?"

"I'm trying to help *you* out."

"Come on, what about my boy?"

"All right, all right. Let me see what I can do."

George brought us food and some other stuff we craved, like candy and cigarettes. He brought us junk and snacks to eat, and made sure we had toothpaste, soap, and all those jailhouse necessities. They were like money in jail. Typically, an inmate would stay there for about three months waiting to be moved. If it hadn't been for George, we would have sat there in Eastern State a lot longer than we did. After only a few days, the following Wednesday, I was on a van headed for Camp Hill.

JUMP

The bus ride to Camp Hill State Correctional Institution took us straight west through mile after mile of rural Pennsylvania. I had rarely ventured beyond West Philly. The scene out the windows was like the backdrop of a movie. We passed through small towns, by farms with fields of corn, by meadows with cows grazing on acres of grass, over two-lane roads that rolled on for miles. Two hours west of Philadelphia the prison bus crossed the Susquehanna River, took a right turn north to the small town of Camp Hill, and pulled inside the prison fence. That fence didn't open again for me for four years.

THE SOUND OF a bugle woke us up every morning. The food wasn't terrible, but it definitely was not like home. In some ways it was not as difficult for me to exist inside because of the order. On the street, there were all kinds of things going on all the time. Jail, in its own regimented way, was more relaxed, less prone to random acts of violence and mayhem. Still, power ruled.

My first day at Camp Hill this inmate came to my cell and asked: "You Larry Miller?"

I said yeah.

"We gon' fuck you up."

He was a guy named Peanut from the Lex Street gang, which happened to be feuding with my Cedar Avenue crew. He and his boys were waiting for me to show up.

"Why don't you go fuck yourself?" I said. "Kiss my ass while you're at it."

When we lined up for the next meal, Peanut and his boys surrounded me. "That's him," Peanut said.

"Yeah, I'm him, motherfucker," I said. "Bring it here."

A guard showed up and told us to shut up and get back in line.

Later that day another dude showed up at my cell and asked: "You Larry Miller?" I was thinking it's the same drill, but it took a turn. The guy's name was Sam, and he had a message from Benny Ball.

The Ball brothers were two of my closest buddies from the neighborhood. We hung. We took care of one another. I had their backs—they had mine. Benny had been at Camp Hill before, but he had been released before I got there.

"Benny sent me to tell you it's gonna be all right," he said. "We got you."

After that, Peanut and his boys never bothered me. I can't say I felt secure—more like managing security under constant threat.

IT MIGHT BE the most unexpected juxtaposition in my life, but it was during my time at Camp Hill that I learned to love books and reading even more.

Once I settled in and realized I could survive, I checked out my options. I was serving time for a murder, but I was still "the Champ," the smart kid who knew how to study and get good grades. They offered us two choices: work or take high school classes. I did both. In the machine shop I learned how to operate a metal lathe. We used to make lamps and stuff like that. But I spent most of my time in class, trying to earn my GED.

Before I got to Camp Hill, one of the old heads at Holmesburg had pulled me aside. "Young boy, you need to use this time to learn shit. You need to read. Never stop reading. That's how you get smart."

That planted a seed. Then, one of the inmates at Camp Hill named Beans took me aside, handed me a book, and said: "You need to check this out."

Beans had handed me Frantz Fanon's *The Wretched of the Earth*. I really dug it. There I was—a seventeen-year-old kid doing time for murder— reading an existential analysis of anti-Black racism. Did I understand every word? Nah. But a lot of Fanon's ideas sunk in. I also read Westerns and whatever came along. Beans and I became tight over books and pushed one another from book to book.

The Three Musketeers. Les Misérables. The Autobiography of Malcolm X. Never got to *War and Peace*. Beans and I would spend half the day in the library. The Camp Hill library was not what anyone would call well stocked. It had a very limited collection. The shelves were almost bare. When a new shipment of books would show up—all used, of course—it was a big deal. Word would go out, and we would grab them as soon as possible. We had established a network of readers and passed books on as soon as we had finished. I loved Steinbeck's *Of Mice and Men* and passed it right to Beans. *The Odyssey*, too.

Lights would go out in the cells at ten o'clock, but the hall light stayed on all night. So if I wanted to read, I'd get right up to the bars, and I'd read by the glow reflecting off the bars, like Malcolm.

And just like Malcolm, I started to get introduced to Islam behind bars. There was an active Nation of Islam group at Camp Hill, but I was not that interested at that time. I did, however, read *Swine Enterprises*, which described how they processed pork and all their diseases. I never ate pork after that.

To pass time, I started taking classes. Running the streets hadn't made me any less smart. I was still a bright kid. Outside of class I used study guides to prepare for the GED tests. But I believe it was all the reading I did that expanded my mind and improved my comprehension, my ability to grasp complicated subjects.

Despite all the reading, English and writing were harder for me. Math always came easier. I breezed through math classes and had no problem with math on the GED test.

I did so well they encouraged me to take courses in computer programming, which the prison had just introduced to the classroom. I was one of the first students, and I did very well.

They would bring inmates who were computer wizards down from different penitentiaries and put them to work for the state of Pennsylvania. That put guys serving time who were also computer masterminds programming computer systems and doing other high-tech jobs for the state. They brought a few of them down to Camp Hill, too.

The office for the headquarters of the Bureau of Corrections for the State of Pennsylvania was at Camp Hill, right across the street from the penitentiary. The prison had created a program where those inmates would put on their state-issued suits and ties, and go out to work at the Bureau of Corrections office every day. The state's systems were just starting to become digitized. Most of that original programming was done by this group of inmates.

When they asked me to be part of the programming group, I put on my little state-issued cheesy suit and tie every morning, went outside the gate and across the street to the office, and worked there all day. I worked that job the whole last year that I was in Camp Hill. It was my first introduction to an office environment. It was a civilian office, and we had our own little area inside of it. We were inmates and everybody there knew it, but we moved around the building freely. And we all had on the same suit and tie.

The main guys in the program were these two sharp, old white guys, Andy and Matt. They were really smart, and cool, too. They taught me programming languages like COBOL and BASIC. And Andy taught me how to play chess. We would sit there all day long and work on computers, then go back into the prison in the evening.

I worked in that program until I went home.

A FEW DAYS after we took the high school graduation test the lead teacher who administered the GED came to my cell.

"How'd I do?" I asked.

"Not only did you pass," he said, "but you got the highest score out of this group. Matter of fact, your scores were some of the highest I have ever seen since I started giving GED tests a decade ago.

"That makes you the valedictorian," he said. "We want you to give a speech during graduation."

"Uh-uh," I said. "That ain't happening."

I was all into my hood image. I didn't want my boys to think I was too smart. "Valedictorian" and "gangster" didn't fit for me. But word got out on the block we were in, and Beans got a hold of me. He and a few others convinced me to do it. When they told me I could invite my family to the graduation, I was all in.

It was not easy to keep my connection to my Philadelphia family. We couldn't use the phone in the warden's office to call out unless we had a damn good reason, so we wrote letters home—maybe a few a year when we needed something. Those calls and letters helped pull me through, kept me whole. My mother continued to show her love and empathy. She wrote often and ended every note with *"As ever, Mom."* But Catherine wasn't about to broadcast my crime and jail time around the neighborhood. She kept that close. Matter of fact, when my older brother, Bill, returned from Vietnam, he kept looking around for me. Bill is about ten years older, but we are still tight. On his second or third day back home, he finally asked: "Hey, where's Larry?"

No one had bothered to tell him that I was serving time for murder.

Mom and Lon came up on family days a few times a year. They would load the car up with my sisters and Ted, a picnic basket full of my favorites—Mom's chicken and potato salad— and make the drive up from West Philly. Of course, guards checked the basket for weapons or drugs, but we expected that. The families were often treated to a talent show. My buddies and I had put together a singing group. Little-known fact: I used to sing back then. We weren't quite the Temptations, but did our best as the "Reputations."

On graduation day, Mom and Lon came with my brother Ted. They watched me deliver my valedictory speech.

I can remember only the last line: "Let's not serve time; let's let time serve us."

Then I joined my little family on the lawn for some decent food. We had a nice lunch on the grassy area inside the fence. I was eighteen years old. I had learned a lot about academic subjects. I had read dozens of books. I had even picked up the rudimentary aspects of computer coding.

But had I learned enough to stay out of trouble and not land back behind bars?

4

THE NATION

*T*wo years later, on a Friday afternoon in April 1970, my taxi pulled up in front of the Miller family home on Catharine Street. I was twenty years old and had been away for more than four years. The row houses looked smaller. My suit was smaller. My shoes needed polish. My Afro was sculpted to my head. I flashed a big grin at the people gathered on the front steps.

"That's Larry," my sister Glo screamed from the doorway. "Larry's home!"

Glo was getting married the next day. We were able to time the wedding so that I could stand with my sister on her special day. My family accepted me with open arms, as if I was returning from a job out of town. I felt right at home and comfortable back in the neighborhood. I had come home to a party.

Yet I had missed so much. The changes had been monumental—for our little community and the world. The Vietnam War was on TV every night. Martin Luther King Jr. and

Malcolm X had been assassinated. Robert Kennedy had been shot dead. I had missed the 1968 riots that had torn up parts of Philadelphia, Detroit, and L.A.

And then there was heroin. It had taken over the neighborhood. It was horrifying.

When I left in 1965, cheap wine was our drug. We would drink Wild Irish Rose and Thunderbird and hang out on the corners. We would hustle up some money and go to the liquor store and buy some wine, then sit around, and that was it. We weren't even smoking weed. Jerry was the first person who could get us some reefer once in a while and it was a big deal. Now there were junkies on every corner nodding out.

When I went to prison, the war in Vietnam was reaching its height, and a lot of brothers were leaving for Southeast Asia. Before the shooting, I asked my mom about going into the service. I was maybe sixteen and she said: "Nope, no way." Back then, if you were seventeen you could go in with parental consent, and at eighteen you could join as an adult. So, first Catherine, then prison, kept me from going to Vietnam. Otherwise, there is no doubt I would have been sent to war.

Brothers went to war, including my brothers Bill and Jerry, to escape the streets. So many didn't come back. Many of those who did return came back with broken bodies, messed up in the head, hooked on heroin—or all three.

While I was at Camp Hill, Mom used to get me subscriptions to newspapers, and I would read the *Philadelphia Bulletin* regularly. It would always arrive at the prison about a week late. One of the things we would always do was look through the paper to see who from around the neighborhood had been killed in Vietnam. There was always a page with pictures and names of soldiers who had died.

That first day back I was walking up Baltimore Avenue, and I ran into this brother named Happy who I knew from the gang.

"Yo, Happy!" I said, "What's up?"

He said, "Yo, Larry! What's going on, man? You just got out? Yo, man let me hold somethin'."

That meant lend him some money.

I said, "Yo, man, I just got out of jail, man. How you gon' hit me up? Let *me* hold something.'"

"Man, you right," he said. "I'm gon' get you, let me get back to you."

Happy was hooked. I could tell by the way he looked and talked. He had the sleepy eyes and that zoned-out demeanor. Everybody around the neighborhood seemed to be addicted.

The day I came home, I was trying to connect with another friend of mine who we called Big Time. He was just coming home from the military the same day. That whole first day out and the day after the wedding, me and Big Time were trying to meet up with each other. People would say "Man, Big Time was just here looking for you."

Big Time overdosed within days of his return. I didn't get to see him until his funeral.

I did my best to stay out of trouble. I tried to stay around the house at night, and I concentrated on all I had learned at Camp Hill. But gradually I let myself get caught up in a lot of the negative things that were going on at the time. My big brother Jerry introduced me to a guy who was selling heroin, and I started dealing. I did try heroin, but it didn't do anything for me. It made me sick. It just wasn't my thing. In the perspective of the streets, that was perfect because I wasn't interested in using what I was selling. So, it was all business.

Speed was my drug of choice. We called it Monster. I've always been pretty laid back, but I like to know what's going on. With heroin, you don't know what's going on around you, you're just zoned out. You wake up and it's over. With speed, I could be up all night. I would stay awake for four or five days. Then I would go home to Catharine Street and stretch out on the couch and sleep hard for about two days straight. Nobody would dare disturb me. They would still sit around, watch TV, whatever, and I would be right there, knocked out. They would warn people, "Man, don't mess with him." They knew if they woke me up or bothered me, I would wake up mean and pissed off.

BUT EVEN BACK then, hustling drugs on the street, I started to have more introspective moments. I always questioned why it was that so many Black folks lived in such terrible conditions, not just in Philly, but all over the world. Growing up in my poor Black neighborhood in West Philly, I was always searching for reasons why life was the way it was for Black people. Why was there so much poverty and despair where we lived? Why weren't there better jobs, better education, opportunities for better lives?

Those questions eventually led me to the Nation of Islam. The Nation answered all of those questions about discrimination and the predicament of the Black man. It was a different time and a much different Nation of Islam. Elijah Muhammad was still alive, Malcolm X was very much part of the scene early on, and the Nation had a major role in the Black Power movement of the day.

My first introduction to the Nation of Islam was in 1965 in the Holmesburg Prison when I was sixteen. In those days, most brothers joined the Nation while they were incarcerated. I had an entire group of friends and associates that I only ever saw when I was in jail, and many of them were joining.

I understood a lot about the Nation of Islam, but I knew I wasn't ready. There was always a large faction of Muslims in jail, and I was familiar with most of them from having pretty much grown up in jail since the age of thirteen. I had read *Message to the Blackman in America* and *How to Eat to Live*, and other books like those. Although I admired the mentality and strength of the brothers and the group as a whole, and I felt their message of self-determination spoke directly to me, I initially resisted joining.

What appealed to me the most was that the Nation seemed to have answers to my questions about why Blacks were living in poverty and couldn't get ahead. The Nation of Islam saying that "the white man" was "the devil" answered that question at the time. As a frustrated and angry young Black man, it made sense to me. And a lot of the brothers who had joined before me, I believe they felt the same way. The white man was the devil, and it was all part of his plan for world domination, and if we continued to let ourselves get caught up in the traps that were laid out for us—drugs and all the other poisons—then we would continue to be in this bad situation. We had to clean ourselves up and be ready for when the mother ship came. Elijah Muhammad's *Message to the Blackman* laid it all out.

The Nation sought to create an ideal movement of proud, self-sufficient Black men and women who helped each other and took care of one another. They were teaching the community about self-respect, unity, and self-reliance. Their motto, "Do for self," said it all. No longer could the Black community afford to wait around for handouts and government favors. We were not waiting around hoping to be treated with equality in this nation. We were creating our own.

Now, while I do think it helped a lot of people clean up their lives, some of the stuff that was being taught was really crazy when you think about it: the stories about Yakub, the big-headed scientist grafting the white "race of devils," and the mother ship that was going to come and take those of us who were in the Nation back to our home in the stars. All that fictional stuff aside, we did learn a lot. I was capable of distinguishing between the way-out parts of the belief system and the education that came with it.

Of course, there were more orthodox Muslims who were practicing Islam as it's actually written in the Qur'an, true Islam as taught by the prophet Muhammad. At the time, we didn't even acknowledge that; Elijah Muhammad was creating his own philosophy and focused on addressing issues specific to Black people in North America.

Nation of Islam members also impressed me with how they

were always so well-dressed and put together. They just looked like they were progressive. Being in the Nation of Islam meant a life free of drugs, alcohol, and other pollutants. I always said that I would never join while I was locked up. From my perspective, it was much easier to live this type of refined lifestyle we called "sol-diering" while locked away in a jail. It would be more of a testa-ment to my level of commitment to join as a free man on the street, to confront the temptations head-on in my normal environment.

ONE DAY, MY friend Carver "Sonny" Dockins talked me and my girlfriend, Yvonne, who I was living with at the time, into go-ing with him to the Nation of Islam mosque on Fifty-Second and Walnut. Sonny D and I grew up together and were in the same gang. He was one of my closest friends. When he joined the Nation, he showed up at our house on Catharine Street and announced: "From now on, you can call me Saleem."

The Imam's name was Minister Stanley. He was a short little brother—but that brother could preach! He threw down! That night I heard a speech that seemed to be written specifically for me. All the things he was saying were things that I was think-ing and feeling, things that I was going through and dealing with right then and there. He was giving me the answers to all my questions.

"Damn," I kept thinking to myself, "he's absolutely right. That's me."

I left there feeling moved and definitely into it, but I still wasn't ready to join the Nation.

The minister talked about how he knew there were listeners in the audience that day that could identify with his words, and how he could feel their inner struggles right at that moment. He said he knew there was someone out there wanting to join the Nation but having difficulty releasing their attachments to their current way of life. He told us to just go ahead and let go, cut off our Afros—because brothers in the Nation were clean-cut, always—and take that first step into our new lives. Yvonne teased. "You mean you gon' cut off all that pretty hair?"

My Afro was no small issue. I was seriously opposed to cutting it off. That was in 1973. I still wasn't quite ready. Yvonne and I were getting high together; that was part of our whole deal. But at the same time, I was getting tired of the lifestyle. I was drifting, wasting my time. I needed a change.

"You know what?" I said to myself one day. "I'm gonna get a job."

One of the other things I had learned at Camp Hill was how to operate lathes, machines used with other tools to cut metal rods into precise dimensions and shapes. I could make all kinds of things out of metal. So, I got a job working at a machine shop. I worked the 4 P.M. to 12 A.M. shift every day. I had my father, Lon, to thank for setting the role model of a man who went to work, punched a clock, and got a paycheck.

No question I was at a moment of transition. I was still getting high on speed and dealing drugs, but I was also becoming more and more intrigued with the Nation and its call for a clean life, centered on uplifting the Black community. I was at the crossroads of conflicting ways of life, being pulled in many directions. While I had a respectable job, the Nation taught that the white man was the devil, and here I was working for a machine shop owned by a white man.

Something had to give.

There was a notorious junky in the neighborhood named Reds. Junkies didn't get any lower than Reds. One night I was hanging out with him, and I thought, "Damn, I'm hanging out with Reds? What the fuck? I gotta cut this shit out. I've hit the bottom of the barrel. I've gotta get myself together."

I always knew right from wrong. There was a line between the two, and I always knew when I was crossing it. I got that from Mom and Lon. They had taught me to have a conscience. There was always a voice inside; I just chose to ignore it too often.

But at least I was aware of right from wrong.

AROUND THE END of 1973, there was another reason I was drawn to a more settled and organized life. My first child, Laila, was about to be born. Her mother, Pearl, was my sister Florence's best friend. Pearl was around our house on Catharine Street more than I was. She was sassy, strong-willed, and very into me. Her family ran a small corner store that sold ice cream and groceries. It had a separate entrance down into the basement of their house, so we called it the "Dugout." Pearl would always spoil us with free ice cream cones and candy.

My time with Pearl was short-lived, and we were no longer together when we realized she was pregnant, but there was no question Pearl would have that baby. We were both excited about having a child. The fact that I was about to become a father also weighed on me and made me want to move away from the street life.

Then, one night after work I met with a friend, Gregory. We sat down at the kitchen table and started to talk about our lives. He was pretty much in the same place mentally that I was. He was into some things and had been trying to clean himself up. He had gotten shot four or five times but had managed to survive. We sat up that whole night talking. We were tired of the lives we had been living. We had both had a lot of exposure to the Nation of Islam, but neither of us had wanted to join yet. It was a Saturday night.

"Let's join tomorrow," I said.

"I'm in," he responded. "Let's make it happen."

That Sunday in the winter of 1973, we walked into the mosque, and I formally joined the Nation of Islam.

EVEN THOUGH WE'D signed on, I was still trying to hold on to some little elements of my old self. I would go to the temple every week, dressed right and on time, but I still had my Afro. I'll never forget how we were sitting there in a meeting and Minister Phillip was talking and said: "We have brothers in here that want to be here with us and we know they want to be a part of the Nation, but you know, if they want to be here with us, then they gotta look like us, they gotta act like us, they gotta dress like us."

I felt like he was talking about me. I came home to Catharine Street from the temple. My brother Ted, a friend of ours named Larry from around the way, and a few other people were there. I said, "I'm ready to cut my hair."

So, Larry says, "If you're for real, I'll cut your hair for you right now."

He lived close by on Cecil Street, and we walked the short distance around the corner to his house. I sat down, and he cut my 'fro off. There was no looking back at that point. Now I was committed.

WHEN I JOINED the Nation, I went in full tilt—hard-core.

I decided I wasn't doing any drug dealing or gangster rolling, or committing any kind of crime. I was leaving all of that alone. My new goal was to be the best member of the Nation, period.

I committed myself to the whole process you had to go through before you got your X. You had to take F.O.I.——Fruit of Islam—classes and learn all these lessons that were called "the Actual Facts." They were basic scientific realities, like the distance from the Earth to the Sun, for example. Then, you had to answer a series of questions and submit certain papers, and wait for your X to come from the headquarters in Chicago. I was at home in the classroom—whether it was elementary school, getting my GED at Camp Hill, or now studying in Mosque Temple No. 12C above the storefront at Forty-First and Westminster Avenue in West Philly.

I wanted my X.

It was a big deal when you finally received your *X*. A lot of brothers never got to that point because they didn't go through the whole process. I did. I studied hard, passed the tests, and made the grade. Each temple had its own listings, and I was the third Larry in our temple, making me Larry 3X. Once I got my *X*, I got my F.O.I. uniform. That was a huge deal. To be able to show up in your F.O.I. uniform, you were the man! It was blue and had a fez cap, or a brimmed hat for some, and it was cool.

When I had my F.O.I. uniform on—that was the shit!

At that early stage in the process we didn't get to take on a Muslim name. The deal was that we would get our *X*s and then be given a Muslim name at some point later. But after the Honorable Elijah Muhammad passed away in 1975, his son, Warith Deen Mohammed, took over, and he decided that brothers and sisters could all take on their Muslim names. He gave some of them names, but others were just allowed to choose their own.

I took the Muslim name Sharif Abdul Rasheed. *Sharif* means "honorable one" in Arabic, but I chose it because it refers to one who keeps order, a sheriff. I aspired to that.

GENERATING CASH WAS one of Mosque Temple No. 12's primary objectives at the time. The Nation was extremely powerful in Philly in those days. Jeremiah Shabazz was the minister of our temple. He was also straight-up in the mix of all the gangster business. The minister always had brothers at his house guarding him (myself included), and for very good reason. We lived in a very violent world. The brothers were at war with criminal networks for a piece of Philly's bubbling drug market. Black men were being gunned down in brutal hits, especially the leaders of various criminal organizations. In one sense, the Nation was one of those criminal organizations, which put Minister Shabazz in grave danger.

Many brothers would revert to their old ways and turn to committing crimes to contribute their share of cash to the mosque. But I refused to go that route—at first, anyway. I started working for the Nation on the sales side. I was selling fish. I was selling *Muhammad Speaks* newspapers, bean pies, you name it. I have always had a natural capacity for sales, and soon I became the top fish salesman in the temple. In those days, sales were door-to-door. I had the skills to sell fish to every person I encountered, every door that opened to me.

Meanwhile, Laila came into the world. It was a time of joy and celebration for me and my entire family. Pearl brought her to the mosque sometimes. But I think it was more about her trying to stay connected with me rather than adopting the Nation's ways or teachings. She read a lot of the material, even changed up her dress and her diet for a while, but ultimately it wasn't for her. The more I got into the Nation, the further we grew apart. In all fairness to Pearl and Laila, family just wasn't important to me at the moment. I was not ready to settle down at that level.

I quit my job at the machine shop and started working on the fish trucks with the Nation full-time. I went to see the brothers and told them straight away: "I want to sell fish." They had around five or six trucks with something like four or five brothers on each truck. We would load them up with frozen fish, and then everybody would cover a different part of the city.

I showed up for my first day and hopped on my truck. This brother named Samuel was the driver and the leader of the crew. He was one of these brothers who would just talk all the time. We were driving down to North Philly and he was talking, talking, talking, and talking. I was just sitting there, not saying anything. Finally, after we rode for a while, he looked back.

"Brother, you kinda quiet," Samuel said. "You know, you got to talk to sell fish, brother. You know, you can't be all quiet out there tryin' to sell no fish. We sell fish on this truck."

"Brother," I said, "I'm saving all my talk for the customers."

We parked the truck, got out, and started canvassing the area. Every door I knocked on was a sale. We were selling fish in ten-pound frozen slabs, and I sold one to every house I went to. Samuel was like, "Damn! I thought the brother was giving the fish away."

I don't know what it was, but I guess I was hot that day. I was in the zone! There was a cat working down inside of a manhole in the street. I bent over it and stooped down to talk to him.

"What you got there, man?" he asked.

"Fish . . ." I said and went into my pitch.

"Naw, I can't, I don't get off until later. What I'm gon' do with it until then?"

"Look here, brother," I said. "This fish is frozen solid. This will last until you get home."

He bought it.

So, that was my thing when I first joined the Nation of Islam.

I was selling fish, selling newspapers, recruiting people, whatever they needed me to do.

We also had a drill team as part of our training. It was run by a brother named Lieutenant Clarence. Myself, my friend Gregory—who had taken the name Seifallah—and a few other brothers who I knew well participated. Every week we would have meetings for all the brothers at the mosque, and the last thing we would do was have everybody fall into formation to do military-style drills. Lieutenant Clarence would call out the cadences, which would get increasingly complicated as he went on. We would have to remember every move. When he gave the order to "March!" we would do the sequence of movements. He would run off a cadence with ten or twelve moves and then say, "March!"

If you messed it up or forgot something, you would fall out, and we would keep it going until the last man was standing. I got really good at it, to the point where I was always one of the last two or three. Then one day I saw this brother named Sylvester who was a lieutenant. I ran into him earlier in the day while we were out selling fish or something, and I said: "Brother Lieutenant, I'm winning the drill tonight."

When we got to the temple later, as soon as we all fell into formation he said: "By the way, I ran into Brother Larry earlier today. He told me that he definitely was gon' win tonight."

"No, Sir. No, Sir," they all chanted.

He looked at me. "Didn't you promise to win tonight, Brother Larry?"

"Yes, sir!" I just claimed it.

I won it that night for the first time. After that, I won every week. I was the last man standing every time. Nobody could beat me. I was the top driller in Mosque No. 12.

At that moment, I was whole. I felt I could be best at whatever I set my mind to: best at selling fish, best at drilling, best at standing tall in my F.O.I. uniform. Joining the Nation, living by its rules, selling its wares, and studying Islam settled me.

As Sharif, I was the proud Black man Elijah Muhammad had envisioned.

5

ARMED AND DANGEROUS

*I*n my first year or so in the Nation of Islam, I would return to the mosque every day after selling fish or bean pies, wearing the customary suit and narrow bow tie. The same dudes would watch me walk through the doors.

"There go that spooky brother," I heard one of them whisper.

Those early days with the Nation I was pretty content and pleased with myself, and wholeheartedly devoted to the faith. I was on the straight and narrow—in other words, the law-abiding path. I was strictly focused on learning about Islam and following the rules of the Nation. I wasn't down for anything criminal.

Some brothers at the mosque referred to members who rolled like that as "spooky," meaning unshakably committed to the religion. I guess that was me at the moment—dedicated to the Nation but staying within the boundaries and rules of the clean-living culture as it was practiced within the mosque.

But the mosque needed cash. Always more money to run its programs. They used those funds to open grocery stores, run health clinics, and operate schools. These were all essential services to a Black community that had been abandoned. Was I contributing my share by selling fish, even if I was the best at it? As time passed, I watched how so many of the brothers who were willing to commit crimes were contributing much, much more money to the Nation than I could on the legitimate side. I wanted to be able to give more.

Even though it wasn't my initial intention, I began to slip back into my gangster life so I could be a more meaningful member of the Nation.

It was an easy transition for me.

LATER THAT YEAR, I went to see Eugene "Bo" Baynes, a notorious gangster. Brother Baynes was basically viewed as the godfather of West Philadelphia. He was reported to have been one of the founding fathers of what became known as Philly's Black Mafia, a group of brothers loyal to the Nation of Islam and Mosque No. 12 who allegedly committed some of the bloodiest acts of violence in Philadelphia history. They left a trail of death and blood across the city back in the 1970s.

Bo owned a corner grocery store on South Fifty-Sixth Street in our West Philly neighborhood. Saleem and I tracked him down there. Saleem went in and told Bo we needed some guidance. We sat in a car parked out front, motor running. He came out, leaned into the open window on the shotgun side, and said: "What can I do for you brothers?"

"Brother Bo," I said, "we want to be able to make more of a contribution to the Nation. We're selling fish, recruiting people, and doing all these things for the Nation."

"That's all good," he said.

"But we've both reached a point where we want to start contributing more money. The only way that we can do that is by getting involved in some other things. What we're doing is cool and all, but we want to start contributing real money."

Bo knew what that meant.

He looked over his shoulder. His eyes swept the back seat. He fixed his glare on me and Saleem. "I know y'all," he said, "and y'all are good brothers. If y'all want to get down, I'll put you down."

We were in.

He leaned farther into the window until his face seemed to fill it.

"I'll put y'all down," he said. "That ain't no thing. But y'all need to understand this. The contribution you brothers are already making is the most valuable thing that anybody can give. You contribute your time. Time is much more valuable than money. Money comes and goes. You can always get more money when it's gone, but when you run out of time, that's it. You can never get more time."

Bo smiled, backed out of the window, and withdrew slowly back to his store.

"Yeah, yeah, we hear you, Bo," we said. "You right."

But we still intended to be down—down with his "businesses."

Bo's words stuck with me, but it took me a while to understand exactly what he meant. I had always felt that I could figure out a way to get some money if I needed it, whether it was getting a job, or whatever. Not long after I had come home from Camp Hill, Mom had gotten me a job at the airport cleaning the terminals. At the time, I was in my early twenties, and I was getting high on speed. I would go to work high, and I would clean the hell out of those terminals! I mean, they would be spotless. The dude who was my supervisor would say, "You are good!"

Once when I'd been out of work, I had gone down to the welfare office. A lot of people around the hood were on welfare and getting food stamps. So, I said, I might as well get down with that. But when the caseworker asked me for all this personal information, I just walked out.

"You know what," I said to myself, "I'm not going through all this crazy stuff and telling them all my business. I'm gonna go get a job."

I left that office and on the way home, I stopped and saw this guy I'd met through my brother Jerry. He was a manager at the Gimbels department store downtown. I got hired that day. I worked there for about a month or so.

So, what Bo was saying was absolutely clear to me: time is more important than money. I still believe I can always get more money. That's why I don't get hung up about it. I've always felt that I could figure out a way to get what I need. Back in the day, if figuring it out meant that I had to put a gun in my hand and stick somebody up, I was gonna figure it out. It was whatever it was. I always believed that I could get more money.

But time? If you waste it, it's wasted. It's gone, and there's no going back and saying: "I'm gonna go add some more time." Or: "I'm gonna take that time back."

That's what Bo Baynes was trying to tell us. It didn't really sink in at the time—but I totally get it now.

ONCE BO PUT us "down," I left the "spooky" brother at the mosque.

My transition back to the criminal side was swift and seamless. I already knew the territory and the players. I started hanging out with the folks who were into the money-making, criminal side of the Nation. I started getting high on speed again. I was selling heroin and running a crew of street dealers. Internally, I was conflicted. As much as I wanted to be a good Muslim, it was easy for me to slip back into what I knew, what I was comfortable with. What I was doing ran counter to the teachings of Allah and Elijah Muhammad, but in service to the local mosque and the needs of the community, making money (legally or illegally) made sense to me and took priority. At that stage in my life the financial needs outweighed the methods. I ignored the conflict it presented for what I saw as the good of the Nation. I swung hard to the criminal side. Too hard.

One of my guys was a brother named Billy. I had known him for years. He grew up in the 5500 block of Catharine Street, right down the block from Mom and Lon's place. I went over to Billy's house to pick up my money, and I didn't even count it. I just left and went home. Now, I had been getting high, which probably played into what happened next. I got home and realized, "This is short. This muthafucka is stiffing me on my money."

So, I stuck my gun in my belt and went back. On my way, I had already decided that I was going to walk in the door, shoot Billy in the leg, and then put the gun to his head and tell him to convince me not to kill him. No way I could abide by him shorting me. I got to his house, and his girlfriend opened the door. Billy wasn't there but he was on his way home.

"I'll wait for him," I said. I settled down on a couch, the pistol still tucked in my belt.

"What's up, Brother Larry?" she asked.

I told her that her man was ripping me off. She started pleading his case. She told me how Billy respected me. That we were longtime friends. That he was honest to the core.

"Billy would never do that to you," she said.

So, I started questioning myself. Now I wasn't certain; I didn't know if I was right in the money count or what. At first I was absolutely certain he was stealing from me. Now I had her in my ear and I had been getting high. I started to waver. By the time Billy got home I didn't know anything for sure. When he walked in the door I said: "Let's go upstairs."

We went up into a room. He closed the door. I pulled the gun.

"I think you're trying to rip me off," I said. "The only reason I didn't shoot you when you walked through the door is because your girlfriend told me that that couldn't be the case, and she's got me questioning my shit, but let me tell you something—if you ever do decide to rip me off, I will blow your fucking head off, Billy. I don't care how long I've known you."

Billy started crying. He was sniveling and begging for his life.

"Brother Larry," he said, "I would never do that—ever. I don't want to sell for you no more."

"No," I said. "You gon' keep selling for me for as long as I want you to, and if you even think about ripping me off, just know that I don't care how long I've known you, I will blow you the fuck away."

I left Billy groveling on the floor, curled up in a ball. His girlfriend gave me a tight smile and hard stare as I walked out of the front door.

On the way home, I started thinking about it all. Billy was somebody who I'd known all this time. Here I was supposedly a Muslim, trying to help Black folks, and I'm out here being *that* dude. Maybe it was the speed wearing off. I felt terrible that I had left this man just about pissing in his pants—for what? His girlfriend's glare stuck with me, too. I stopped on the corner of Fifty-Second and Pine, not far from where I had shot the boy back when I was sixteen. I felt so small and disgusted with myself at that moment. I told myself that I just couldn't do this anymore.

I decided at that point to stop selling drugs. I was going to figure out another way to get money.

That was when I started doing stickups.

THE FIRST FEW jobs I did were with Seifallah—the brother who joined the Nation with me. Seifallah and I had committed to one of the lieutenants that we would bring in a certain amount of money by the next day. So, we knew we had to go out and get that amount of money. He and a couple other brothers from the drill team were already doing stickups. My first one was a McDonald's in South Philly. We got away with a nice chunk of money—maybe five or six grand. We split it up, and then I went and bought a couple of new suits and gave the rest of the money to the Nation.

We were primarily robbing white folks in their businesses, which made it okay in our eyes, or at least better than selling drugs to neighbors. That was how I justified it back then. I always carried a semi-automatic pistol jammed into my belt under a jacket. It was a tool of the trade. Just as I applied myself to being the best fish seller in the mosque, I applied myself to the art of the stickup: not hurting anyone and getting away with wads of cash.

Then I hooked up with two older guys who had been working with a few different crews in West Philly. They set up stickups and would never do the jobs themselves. Think of them as the CEO and CFO; they would do all the strategizing and reconnaissance work. One of the guys would always stress to us that money always has to leave an establishment—somehow. So, he would sit, watch, and figure out how the money left a particular place. Then he would plan the best way to pull it off.

We'd get stolen cars, he would provide the guns, then me and a brother named Latif would do the stickups. We had a nice little roll going. We were mainly doing supermarkets and similar small businesses. We would wait and watch as he would show us how the people would come to pick up the money or bring it to a night drop.

We had a routine with McDonald's where we would wait until they were closing and hide out in the back. When the manager and the workers were coming out at the end of their shift, we would jam them up, take them back inside, and make them open the safe and get the money. Then we would tie them up and leave them.

I recall unloading wheelbarrows full of cash at Mosque No. 12. Brothers back then were of a mindset that we would do anything to protect and uphold the Nation of Islam and the Honorable Elijah Muhammad. No guilt, no remorse, no second thoughts.

Later on, I came to understand that some of the things that the Honorable Elijah Muhammad was teaching were not reality. However, he taught some of us things we needed to hear in order to see ourselves differently. I understand that the white man is not "the devil." "The devil" could be anybody. I understand all of that now, but at the time the Nation helped me because it gave me purpose. Before that, my purpose was the gang. When it was no longer the gang, I didn't have any purpose at all. The Nation of Islam became my purpose.

FORTUNATELY, I WASN'T involved in the more notorious and violent acts that Bo Baynes and some of the other brothers allegedly committed. But I surely would have been had I had the opportunity.

I understand what their perspectives were: all in, all or nothing for the Nation, control the streets and the street trade. While a lot of that gunplay and carnage was going on, I was selling fish and selling papers. By the time I finally started to get into that side of the Nation, a lot of the familiar names like Sam Christian, Robert "Nudie" Mims, Ronald Harvey—the more notoriously violent leaders—were getting busted and had started serving long sentences. Bo Baynes was arrested shortly after he brought us in.

When Elijah Muhammad passed away in 1975, Warith Deen Mohammed took the lead and began to take the Nation in a totally different direction, more in the direction of what Islam is really about. Then, at a certain point, as Louis Farrakhan rose in power, he disagreed with the direction the Nation was taking, and there was another split.

Warith Deen Mohammed's group became known as the American Muslim Mission in 1978. That same year, Farrakhan began heading up the Nation of Islam. Members of Mohammed's organization recognized themselves as Americans who were also Muslims, who prayed and fasted, and lived in accordance with the Qur'an. That was where I was most comfortable. When Warith Deen Mohammed took over he brought us out of that whole "white man is the devil" rhetoric, and really started to teach the true meaning of Islam. That's where I landed. That's where I am today—a practicing Muslim.

IN THOSE DAYS there was a tremendous power of intimidation that came with being a member of the Nation of Islam, and we used it to the benefit of the mosque. The news would always have reports saying "be on the lookout for well-dressed Black men in a late-model sedan" being at the scene of some crime.

I was one of those guys. Besides robbing small businesses, we were also extorting money from drug dealers and folks that were committing various crimes. We would tell them: "Okay, you're gonna have to break bread with the Nation." And the proceeds would all go to the mosque.

Take Cody Blue. Blue was a guy from Cedar Avenue, from our gang, who became a pretty big-time hustler. He was into everything. You name a criminal enterprise, and Cody Blue was doing it. I grew up with him.

Seifallah, Saleem, and I were discussing how Cody Blue needed to start supporting the Nation. We had been trying to track him down for a while. He knew it, so he kept ducking us. One night he was throwing a cabaret at a place down on North Broad Street. We knew he would be there, so we decided we would go down there and step to him. We didn't need guns because there was so much fear associated with the Nation of Islam that we felt we could go unarmed and extort a major hustler based solely on reputation.

We were driving somebody's old bombed-out car. It was so bad that we had to park it around the corner and walk. We knew we couldn't pull up in front of the place in that and pretend we were tough guys. We walked in the door where they were collecting money.

"We ain't paying," I told the person at the door, "we came here to see Cody Blue."

Our faces were stone cold. They did not object.

I saw Cody Blue across the room. We headed directly toward him and all the people surrounding him backed slowly away from him. They thought we were coming to blow his brains out.

When he realized we had cornered him, his head just sank down low on his shoulders.

Some guy who knew me walked up trying to start a conversation.

My mindset was so focused that I wasn't even trying to hear anything else right then. I walked up to Blue. No handshake. No smiles. No chichat.

"You know we've been looking for you," I said, "and you know what it's about. I'm gonna come see you tomorrow and were gonna sit down and figure out how you're gonna support the Nation of Islam. This ain't a discussion and this ain't no negotiation. That's what's gonna happen."

I told him I'd be by at a certain time tomorrow. After I laid it out for him, we turned around and walked out. When we got back to the car, we busted out laughing.

"Do you believe what we just did?" Saleem said.

We had nothing, but we walked in and bluffed it. I'm sure Cody's boys were armed, but we didn't care. After that, every week I would pick up Cody Blue's donation to the Nation of Islam. He and I remained friends. He understood that it wasn't personal.

THEN MY TIME came.

Latif and I had a routine for sticking up places in our

neighborhood, and we had expanded out into South Philly, too. But we were running out of targets. Latif had an idea.

"What about we try some places out in the suburbs, just over the city line?"

"Just over the city line" were the wealthy, low-crime suburbs of Montgomery County. Being from West Philly, we didn't know much about the area, but it was close, and it was jammed with juicy targets. Within a week or two we hit a few supermarkets and fast-food joints.

Things were going well until we stuck up a supermarket after closing. Someone was still inside and tripped the alarm. Latif and I sprinted for our ride, but it was too late. The cops showed up and *boom*—they cuffed us and drove us to the local precinct.

I wasn't too worried, since we hadn't really done anything. I figured they didn't have much evidence. At the police station I gave the cops an alias. I used the name of a guy in my gang, Earl Jefferson, who had never been busted before. I had never been busted in Montgomery County, so when they ran my fingerprints through their system, nothing came up.

Whew. I was already contemplating how to get back home when this big, white Montgomery County cop strolled over and sat down next to me. He looked me up and down and smiled.

"Now, I cannot believe that you've never been arrested before," he said. We locked eyes. It was as if he could feel it in his gut, or his bones, or something. "I just can't believe that."

"Hey, you ain't got no record on me," I said, "so . . ."

"I just can't believe that," he said. "I'll be back."

This dude took my fingerprints and drove to Philadelphia police headquarters and ran them again.

I was sitting in the cell when he came back.

"Earl Jefferson, huh?" he said. "Try Larry Miller."

He started running down my rap sheet.

"You're not going anywhere," he said. "Make yourself comfortable."

I was still on parole at the time, and they put a detainer on me to hold me. That was it. I was done.

The Montgomery County cops connected me to four more stickup cases. They brought in witnesses and victims and put me in lineups. Over and over, after each lineup, the cops kept hearing: "Yeah, that's the guy."

By the time they were done they had evidence to bring charges against me in at least five robbery cases.

THE MONTGOMERY COUNTY jail was right across the street from the courthouse in Norristown. Every morning I would get dressed, they would handcuff me, and then two sheriffs—one white and one Black—would come over and walk me over from the jail to the courthouse. They would stay there at the courthouse to watch me all day and then walk me back to jail.

On the first day of the trial, the white sheriff and I got into a huge argument. It was heated, and I don't even remember what it was about, but we were going at it.

"Man, fuck you! Take these handcuffs off me, and I'll kick your ass!"

He was like, "Yeah, all right. I'll take 'em off. Come on!"

He was ready to go.

The Black sheriff was trying to cool everything down, but as they were walking me back to the jail, I was cussing the white sheriff out the whole way.

"Yeah, punk-ass muthafucka, let me catch your ass in the street." I'm going off on him. And he's giving it right back to me.

That night I was laying in my cell thinking about that whole thing. Then I came to a realization. I couldn't win this, there was just no way. I was handcuffed, literally. This was a no-win situation for me. He had the upper hand. But I had to find a way to take control and make it work for me in any way possible.

The next morning, I got dressed and I walked out. The same two guys were there ready to escort me to court. The white sheriff was pumped up and ready to pick up where we left off the day before. He was in battle mode. I could see it all over him. I walked up to them, looked him dead in his eyes.

"Good morning," I said. I smiled and nodded, as if we were meeting for breakfast at the local diner.

The white sheriff looked at me real strange.

"How you feeling today?" I asked. "I feel a whole lot better than I did yesterday, how about you?"

He said, "Yeah, me too."

I said, "Cool."

For the rest of my court cases, this white lawman was eating out of my hand. He even got in trouble for bringing me food and allowing my family to visit me when they weren't supposed to. I was thinking to myself: "I'm still gone kick your ass if I see you in the street, but you don't need to know that because you got the upper hand right now."

This incident taught me about using my head rather than my fists to control myself in tense situations. The sheriff, still ready to go to battle the next day, was completely caught off guard with my pleasant demeanor. I could cuss him out and fight him, but there was no way I could win. I realized that by corralling my anger I was able to take control. I have recalled that episode throughout my career.

I had flipped the script on him. Even in cuffs and headed for jail time, I notched that as a win.

I WAS CAUGHT, but not convicted. Though they had evidence linking me to five robberies, I managed to maneuver my way out of the worst cases.

A few of the cases were thrown out, thanks in part to Latif. My partner was cool through the whole thing. He had never been busted before, and they kept trying to get him to turn on me. They wanted him to say that I was the guy making him do all this, and that I was the mastermind and all that, but he wouldn't do it. They were telling him that he could get out if he talked, but he wouldn't give me up. He ended up getting sentenced to three to ten years.

One of those cases was for a robbery in Montgomery County, and yeah, we did it. It happened on my sister Leen's birthday. She had a big party that night. I did go to the party—after we did the robbery. Leen, my brother-in-law Ronnie, my sister-in-law

Vera, and a few other people all testified truthfully that they had seen me at the party. I used that as my alibi, and the jury found me not guilty.

In another case the jury found me guilty, but the judge gave me concurrent sentences. I had gotten four to ten years for one of the robbery cases, and I was already serving that time. For the second case, the judge gave me three to ten years running concurrently. That means that for all those armed robberies, I ended up with four to ten years.

But hanging over my head the whole time was the homicide I had committed when I was sixteen. The new charges and convictions put me in jeopardy of serving out the full twenty-year sentence for homicide. The homicide plea I had taken carried a minimum and a maximum. I had to do at least four and a half years, and then I could apply to make parole. The Pennsylvania Parole Board could either let me go in four and a half, or they could make me stay and finish out any amount of time up to the twenty, depending on any kind of trouble I may have gotten into while in jail. Because of good behavior in Camp Hill, once my minimum was up, I went in front of the parole board, and after my four and a half years—during which I scored so well on my GED—the board granted my release, but this meant that when I got out, I still had fifteen and a half years remaining on parole.

Typically, if somebody gets convicted for a new crime, no matter how long they've been on the street, the time left on parole is added onto their total sentence. In other words, even though I had been out for about five years or so, when I got convicted for these new crimes, I went back to having that fifteen and a half years of parole time hanging over my head. They could have made me do fifteen and a half years and *then* start my new sentence, with a maximum of ten years. I was looking at being locked up for twenty-five years. That meant a life behind bars until I was in my fifties.

The decision of how much time I would serve was up to the five-member Pennsylvania Parole Board. I had one chance to plead my case for a reduced sentence, both for the prior case and the armed robberies. No lawyer, no advocate: just me arguing for my future. At minimum I figured I would have been lucky to serve about five years of the remaining fifteen.

I was nervous the morning the representative of the board heard me out. But I had had time to organize my thoughts and prepare to make the best case. I was facing jail time, but I surely didn't want it to become decades. I thought about what I had learned from all the books I had read. I thought about the classes I had taken at Camp Hill. I thought about Laila, my toddler. Corrections officers walked me into a small meeting room. The representative from the board was seated at a table; dressed in prison clothes, I faced him alone, without counsel.

"Mr. Miller," he asked, "why should you not have to serve your full sentence and time remaining from Camp Hill?"

I looked at him squarely.

"Speaking of Camp Hill, I believe some of my finest days were studying, learning how to code computers, and graduating at the top of my class," I said. "I intend to pick up where I left off, continue my education, and become a contributing member of society."

We went back and forth. He asked about my family. I was able to talk about how Mom and Lon were role models, and I was committed to regaining their trust and making them proud. And I told him I wanted to become a good father and help raise Laila. The half-hour interview flew by in a blink. He thanked me and told me that I would hear something back within a few weeks. The corrections officer led me back to the holding cell.

Less than a week later the parole officer called me into a meeting room off the cell block. I sat down across from him, with a corrections officer watching from the door.

"The board ruled you have to do nine months of your back time on the homicide," he said. I almost couldn't believe it. By that point I had almost nine months in jail already after being in the county jail for six months, waiting to go to court, and getting sentenced. That might have been why they went easy on me. They let the time that I had done up to that point count for my previous sentence and allowed me to move forward and begin the next one. It was a total blessing.

Again, another one of those lucky breaks. For all those robberies and the back time from the homicide, I would end up serving a total of four years and nine months in the state penitentiary— period. Incredible! I was blown away. I tried to keep cool in front of the parole board clerk and the corrections officers.

6

LEARNING TO SURVIVE

When the metal door slid shut at Graterford State Penitentiary in 1976, my reaction was different from every other time I had been in jail: "I'm getting out of here as soon as possible and never coming back. I'm done."

By then I was twenty-seven and knew the drill. Lining up for cafeteria food, the exercise in the yard, the loneliness of the cell at night. I was tight with a number of inmates. So many had come from the same West Philly streets. Many shared the Muslim faith.

One morning I was shoveling out breakfast as part of my kitchen job. This huge brother stops in front of me and says: "Can I have some more? I'm hungry this morning."

I was working shoulder to shoulder with Brother Wazir, aka Freddie Butler. As soon as I landed at Graterford, I connected with Wazir. He was smart, committed, humble, learned, trustworthy, and positive—always a positive influence. We met in

E block and lived three cells away from one another. From my first days in, Wazir was my road dog, my walkie. To the extent I survived, even thrived, at Graterford and came out whole, it was thanks to Brother Wazir and others who guided me through, offered up sound advice, and had my back.

Wazir looked at the big dude, looked at me without speaking, didn't nod, and kept dishing out eggs.

"Gotta ask the guard," I said. Rules.

The guard was a tall, skinny white guy. Decent officer, always pleasant and respectful. He was standing behind me. The inmate asked him about seconds. He shook his head and said: "Nope, keep it moving."

The inmate sat down at his table and placed the tray gently in front of him, but he never put a fork in the food. He stared straight ahead. He turned around and looked at the guard, got up from his table, walked over, and punched him in the face. He hit him so hard, the force lifted the guard off his feet. He landed straight on the hard floor, head first, as if he had been dropped from the ceiling. Watching from the kitchen, I could tell that the guy was gone. He died on the spot.

The inmate ran up to his cell and armed up with two shanks. Guards rushed him, wrestled him to the ground, and put him in the hole. Wazir actually saw him later and was able to talk to him.

"Man," he told Wazir, "I didn't mean to kill the guy."

They kept that inmate down there for a couple of years, and that was where he died.

I hardened myself to that kind of daily threat of death, but

I knew this life was no longer for me. How could I turn it around?

I never doubted my smarts. I reminded myself I was still "the Champ," the kid who had aced tests in elementary school. I was the teenager who read *The Autobiography of Malcolm X* at night by the hall light in my cell at Camp Hill. I earned my GED with ease—even earned valedictorian.

Alone in my hard bunk the night the guard was killed I made myself a promise: I was done with the cycle of violence that kept landing me here. "I am gonna learn my way out."

GRATERFORD STATE PENITENTIARY was thirty-five miles northwest of Philadelphia, surrounded by small rural Pennsylvania towns like Collegeville, Pottstown, and Blue Bell. Even before I made the bus ride to the wall, I had checked out the prison's educational opportunities.

At that time the state of Pennsylvania had developed full-fledged, vigorous education-release and work-release programs. Going back to its earliest days under William Penn, the state had encouraged work and education in its prisons. In 1965, President Lyndon Johnson signed the Higher Education Act, which made inmates eligible for Federal Pell Grants to support college courses. In the political climate of the 1970s, many states across the country had adopted hearty, well-funded programs to help people behind bars prepare for their lives after prison—either with work release, education programs, or both. Pell Grants were essential.

Graterford allowed inmates to take classes at colleges outside the penitentiary—but first you had to serve at least half your minimum sentence. For me that meant two years and nine months. And I also had to earn a certain number of credits at classes within the prison.

"Damn," I told Wazir, "that's for me: earn credits inside and go to school outside as soon as possible."

Wazir agreed. He was also all about using his prison time to educate himself.

The fact that Graterford had an entire education wing of classrooms and a library blew me away. I walked into the halls one day, looked around at the classrooms and the books, and just about cried. "A safe place to get an education and all the time to study," I thought. Local colleges and universities set up classes for inmates. Professors came from Villanova University, Temple, Cheyney, Montgomery County Community College. Standing there, I started to feel a sense of hope and a sense of purpose. If I successfully completed the program, I could reduce my jail time and be released earlier.

In my first week behind bars I gathered all the lists of courses, studied the class schedules, and figured out how many I could take and still fulfill my work duties in the kitchen. I had barely settled in and gotten my bearings with old friends when I started schoolwork. I took courses in English, math, history, social studies—whatever they offered. I was comfortable with the textbooks and took the lectures seriously. I filled notebooks with highlights from classes and added new ideas. When professors asked questions, my hand shot up. I scored well on tests.

Just like in grade school, I was the teachers' favorite.

Every morning I would wake up before dawn and dig into the assigned reading or work on math problems. When the morning buzzers sounded for breakfast, I would put on my brown uniform and sandals, join the line down to the cafeteria, and work my shift in the kitchen. As soon as we cleaned up, I was off to the education wing. I had to work three shifts in the kitchen. Class might last all afternoon and into the evening. I might get some exercise after class, but mostly I studied, read assignments, and went to the mosque.

It all started as a way for me to try to get out. At first, I didn't think that I was ever going to be able to use all that schooling or make anything out of it. It was a way to get out sooner due to the way the program was structured. That was why I got into it.

Islam also motivated me to change. My religion helped me to focus on living my life in a better way. Before I got locked up, I had begun my transition from Elijah Muhammad's practice of Islam to the more traditional teachings of Warith Deen Muhammed. I grounded myself in the Five Pillars of Islam. In Graterford I had more time to study the Qur'an, and I was able to pray five times a day. We joined together every Friday for Jumma. If I was truly trying to be a Muslim, I had to practice the religion, adhere to its basic beliefs, and change my life. I became Brother Sharif not just in name, but in the way I lived my life.

Brother Wazir was crucial to that connection. He was studying to become an Imam, teaching himself Arabic, and bringing me along with him. Physically, Wazir isn't a large man, but his presence could fill up the entire room. He isn't a loudmouth, but his profound yet unpretentious words have always stuck with me. His wisdom and his honesty have helped me stay on my path over the years.

The more I got into my studies, the more I started to believe that perhaps I could change my life. I began to believe that maybe I could accomplish something truly positive. Maybe I could get an education here and try something different. So, I committed myself even more.

Did I convert in a day from the dude sticking up supermarkets to the student lugging around economics textbooks? No. But over the course of the first few months I could feel the pull of learning and the success at mastering subjects, like accounting. I began to believe I could do this education thing. I have never done anything half-assed. I was locked in.

Some of the brothers noticed the change. They knew me as a stickup guy who had served time for murder. Now I'm all up in college. Coming back from class one day, I passed the cell of Omar, a buddy from jail.

"Yo, Sharif," he said.

"What's up, O?" I asked.

"Man," he said, "you must be the smartest muthafucka in the world. Every time I see you, you got a pile of books under your arms."

"No, I'm not, O," I responded. "But I'm tryin' to be. I'm tryin' like hell to be."

MY FIRST CHILD, Laila, was two years old when I started my four-year bit in Graterford. Her mother, Pearl, and I got closer when

I returned to West Philly after serving time in Camp Hill for the murder rap. She tried hard to become part of my life. Even when I went off to Graterford for armed robberies, Pearl didn't give up on me.

Every month or so Pearl would dress Laila up in her finest, drive thirty-five miles northwest from Philly, and show up for family visiting day. Laila got to know her daddy dressed in a prison-issue brown button-down shirt and brown pants. After sitting a while on wooden benches in the dank waiting room of a penitentiary built in 1929, they would join me for an hour or two in the small, outdoor family area—still inside the high walls and barbed wire.

There were other families and children visiting, laughing, talking, taking pictures. My buddies all agreed: "Laila looks just like you."

She's lived with that her whole life. And knowing there was a little girl out there who looked like me only added to my desire to use education as a way out.

THE MORE I got into economics and literature, the more I fed off my own success. Professors rewarded my abilities and hard work with good grades. They were committed to the program, to interacting with inmates and helping them learn. They treated us like inquisitive, motivated students—because we were. They respected us, and we respected them.

Slowly but surely, I had changed.

"Okay," I started to think, "I believe I can do this when I get out of here."

Some inmates could qualify for a furlough program that would let us out to go home for short visits. When I first heard about it, I thought: "How's that going to work? You mean, they're gonna let me go home, and I'm supposed to voluntarily turn myself in and come back here?"

In fact, having a successful furlough was part of the step-by-step release program. First, the free weekend out of jail, then education release. It sunk in that I could get out of jail for a few days, for real. I was motivated to make myself eligible by serving part of my sentence, staying out of trouble, and not getting written up. I applied as soon as I could. For my first furlough, Lon and my sister Glo came up to Graterford to pick me up and drove me home for the weekend. Simple.

No, I was not greeted by a parade or anything special when I showed up in West Philly for that first weekend out. The family was happy to see me, though. Mom gave me a big hug when she got home from work at the airport. We all got together for a meal or two. Then I rolled through my old neighborhood to visit with some friends. "You out?" one brother asked. "I didn't know you were home."

Being in and out of jail, getting locked up and getting out, was a fact of life in my West Philly. It had been my life. Sadly, it was knitted into the fabric of our community.

"Nah, I'm not out yet," I responded. "I'm just out on furlough."

"Cool."

Sunday night Lon delivered me back to jail.

Was I tempted to get back into the life? No way. I was on

a different course. And doing dumb shit was not part of the plan.

FROM THE OUTSIDE, Graterford looked like most prisons: two-story brick buildings grouped in wings and surrounded by a tall, chain-link fence topped by barbed wire, and beyond that is the wall. What set it apart were the trailers. Just beyond the wall and the fencing and the barbed wire, more than a dozen metal housing units sat next to one another, like a little trailer park on the prison grounds. Inside, nothing special—just open rooms with cots or bunks. But no bars.

For me and the other prisoners inside Graterford, being able to live just beyond the wall meant freedom. Not total freedom, but a life outside the walls, literally. It would be my first taste of release. If I could fulfill my course requirements and serve half of my time, I could apply to live in the trailers and start my life of learning outside. Every morning I could leave for college classes and jobs, and return every night. The system of release was based on trust. Had I earned it?

By the spring of 1978, I was ready to apply. With letters of recommendation from counselors and teachers, I put in for education release. I got an extra push from Carol Altenor, Montgomery County Community College's counselor, who worked with inmates to prepare them for release. She and two professors vouched for my work and commitment to the program. On my first try, the prison board accepted my application.

"Cool" was all Brother Wazir said.

We were not big into celebrating, more into moving forward to achieve the goal of getting out. It wasn't long before Wazir was living in the trailers as well, but he was with a few trusted lifers who were tilling fields, raising vegetables, and herding cattle on Graterford's farm. He was working toward commutation. Wazir was in for murdering a man in Norristown in 1968. He had been sentenced to life but had built a commendable, problem-free record behind bars. He felt he deserved to be set free on commutation, so that was his route, rather than a release program.

MY PROFESSORS AND counselors had helped me transfer credits and sign up for classes at Montgomery County Community College in Blue Bell, about a twenty-minute drive from Graterford. I started classes on the Blue Bell campus in the summer of 1978. I also had gotten part-time jobs through the work-release program, often all the way down in Philly. Without Carol's help, I never would have been able to get organized and pull all this off. I had to make a new life, from buying clothes, to setting up bank accounts, to figuring out classes and credits, to staying connected to the prison's Muslim community.

My schedule was complicated and totally dependent on getting around by car. There were forty of us living in the trailers on release, and we shared cars, perhaps six or seven among us. We had to leave the trailers at eight o'clock every weekday morning, drop off inmates at the train station in Norristown so they could get down to jobs in Philly, get to campus in Blue

Bell, get to classes and the library, return to Norristown to retrieve the guys on work release, and make it back to the trailers by 8 P.M.

For the first few weeks, I was paired up with this guy who'd been able to buy a car, but he was a terrible driver and I didn't trust that he would get us all where we needed to go and back. On top of that, he was always trying to leave certain guys behind. I arrived back at the trailers one night and got with Wazir.

"I'm falling out with this dude," I told him. It wasn't the classes at Montgomery College that worried me, or the jobs. "If I don't figure out a better way to get around, I'm not going to make it."

"You should talk to Jabbar," Wazir suggested.

Jabbar, as in Imam Amin Abdul Jabbar, the Muslim leader within Graterford. Jabbar as in Robert "Nudie" Mims. Before he got to Graterford and attained Imam status, Nudie Mims was said to have been one of the most feared and notorious leaders in Philly's Black Mafia. He was infamous for allegedly committing violent acts, disrupting court, and getting away with it. At Graterford he was doing time for allegedly holding up Dubrow's furniture store in 1971, beating up a bunch of people in the store, killing one person, and torching the place. For the twenty-one years Jabbar was in Graterford, he essentially ran the penitentiary. The total prison population was about 3,600, and 1,800 were Muslim. That gave Jabbar control over half of the inmates and control over virtually everything that went on in the prison. In trade for keeping the peace, the warden and guards left Jabbar alone.

We Muslims would gather in Graterford's church to meet and hold our prayer sessions. That was not good enough for Jabbar, who had arrived at Graterford in 1976 after serving in a few other prisons. One Sunday he brought us all down to the basement under the church. He looked around and held out his arms as if to embrace the space, to welcome us to our new home.

"We gon' build a mosque down here," he announced.

We all looked around at the dank, dark basement. Where Jabbar saw a mosque, we saw a smelly room and rats.

"How?" one brother said.

Jabbar was an enormous brother, about six foot seven. He didn't play. He came off as a very nice dude, the type of brother who, as long as you were cool with him, you were all right. But you did not want to get on his bad side. He and I were tight.

He said it again, a little louder and definitive: "We gon' build a mosque down here." He looked around at every brother and stared them in the eye to make sure they'd gotten his point.

Then Jabbar went to the prison authorities and convinced them to let us build a mosque there. Then he reached out to his various connections and got all the money, material, and resources we needed.

The result was nothing short of amazing. It was the first time in the nation that a mosque had been built and funded by inmates. It was a beautiful mosque, with cozy prayer rugs and soft lighting, bright colors and Islamic symbols on the walls, plenty of Islamic texts. Imam Warith Deen Mohammed himself donated the lavish green wall-to-wall carpet. That was where the brothers all hung out. I spent all my time either in that mosque or at school.

AFTER BROTHER WAZIR suggested I speak with Jabbar, I went into the *masjid* and told Jabbar about my problems with the driver. He was well aware that I was in education release, living in the trailers, and on course for full release.

"Well," Jabbar asked, "what'chu need?"

"What I need is to get my own car."

"And how much money would you need to get a decent car?"

"I could probably get a little something for . . . maybe a thousand dollars or so."

Jabbar wrote me a check from the *masjid* for $1,500 on the spot. I went out and bought a car, got insurance, and then became a driver. I'll never forget that, how he helped me. It was essential to my success.

Jabbar had so much power at Graterford—too much—that they moved him out of there. He wound up at another federal prison in Minnesota.

But I'll never forget what he said when he handed over that check: "If that's what you want, don't let anything or anybody stand in the way of your getting an education."

I USED JABBAR'S check to buy a very used 1970 Chevy Nova. We ran that car all over the countryside.

Same drill—we would pile into our cars to leave at eight

o'clock in the morning, and we had to be back by eight that evening. Now that I was behind the wheel, driving to school, going to work, living out in the trailers, it was smoother. Every day I would ride with another brother named Fred. We were the only ones on education release going to Montgomery County Community College, then to part-time jobs; everybody else was going straight to work. There were many nights when Fred and I would be leaving our jobs in Philly, after classes in Blue Bell, thinking, "Damn, we ain't gon' make it in time."

I would be speeding like crazy. Then we'd get to Norristown and pick up inmates who had come with us in the morning. I would turn my cap around to the back and say: "All right, hold on." Fred knew that that meant we were about to burn. I'd be dipping in and out of lanes, staying ahead of traffic. I wouldn't even look at the clock. Fred would keep time for me. I'd say, "Fred, how we doing?" and he'd say: "We good, just keep doing what you doing."

And we always made it. We never got busted. Sometimes we just made it, pulling up at 7:59, but we were never late. Then I studied. Then I tried to sleep for a few hours. Then we would begin again the next morning.

ARRIVING ON CAMPUS and showing up to class was a trip in itself. I was a felon on a mission to get out of jail among a student body of recent high school graduates and young professionals trying to get a leg up.

Montgomery County Community College, or Montco, was

founded in 1964 to provide a two-year program that offered associate degrees, kind of a stepping-stone to a four-year program for commuting students. Its first campus was in Conshohocken, closer to Philly. In 1972, it opened a new campus on 168 acres of farmland in Blue Bell, between Philly and Graterford. It was a lovely campus with buildings that still felt new when I arrived there in 1978.

I tried to look like a college student. Every morning I put on khakis, a button-down shirt, and sneakers, and carried a backpack. Initially, I thought that I could handle it, but coming from the penitentiary to go to classes after not having been in school for so long, I had some doubts about my ability to keep up. But I was able to knock out the classes easily.

English, economics, history, biology, accounting—whatever the subject, I did well. Top of the class. I finished up my first semester with a 4.0 grade point average. When I got straight As that first semester, I started to connect with some of the teachers. Most of them didn't know my whole deal. They just thought I was a regular student like everybody else. Since it was a community college, there were plenty of other older students there. I didn't really stand out in that respect.

Many of the teachers I had back then were very supportive. Dick Greenwood was an English teacher and also the coordinator and manager of the prison program at Montco. He was the sponsor of the program, and we were required to check in with him from time to time. I met him while I was still inside; he used to come in and teach classes now and then. We became friends. When I came out and started taking classes on the campus, he was an advisor for me and the other guys in Graterford's education-release program. Greenwood took me under his wing.

I wound up connecting to a bunch of professors.

I'd gotten to be cool with the teacher who taught my real estate classes, which I took so I'd be qualified to take the exam for a real estate license. I took that first class as an elective. It was taught by Professor Valentino Pasquarella. He was a big Italian dude, one of these guys who did not play in class. I had seen him jump right on people's cases in class, but he and I just clicked. He took a liking to me because I was always on point, had my homework, answered questions, stuff like that. We called him "Big Val," and he and I got to be good friends.

At first Big Val didn't know what my deal was. I stayed after class one day, and we were talking, and I told him that I was in education release from Graterford. He could have been turned off, but he really started looking out for me. I took the second real estate class, so then I could take the exam. I ended up doing a little bit of work for his appraisal company. He wanted to teach me the real estate business, so I would hang out and go on different jobs with him, kind of like an apprentice. He really looked out for me.

One of the best science professors was a Black man. He came from a whole family of scientists, and he was rumored to be the great-great-grandnephew or something of George Washington Carver. He was another person there who was really encouraging and helpful to me all along the way.

My courses covered a variety of subjects, but I focused on

business. The way I decided to lay it out was to take only classes that could transfer to a four-year college. That way, if I decided to go for my bachelor's degree I would already have a head start. Carol helped me work this all out when she was my counselor. When I started going to classes on the Montco campus, she and I linked up and started hanging out personally. She was instrumental in helping me lay out my academic path.

I worked in the computer lab for a little while tutoring students because I was there taking computer classes so often. Around 1979, I decided to major in computer programming. But then I took an accounting class, in part because Accounting I and II were required. I enjoyed them. The guy who taught both Accounting I and II was a good teacher, and he and I also clicked.

One of the accounting professors knew my situation because her husband was involved with the education-release program at Graterford, helping with coordinating. I went to talk to her and told her that I was thinking of majoring in accounting.

"I like it," I told her, "and I'm pretty good at it so far. I like to make things balance."

"You know," she said, "based on your situation, if you got your bachelor's degree in accounting, and you had to take a clerk's position, just to get your foot in the door somewhere, you should do that."

But for me that meant starting out in a position that didn't require a degree, and that was beneath me. Was she limiting my professional trajectory because of my race, or because I was an inmate? I didn't care. I wasn't buying it.

"No, Professor," I said, "that's not how I see it."

I figured if I put in the same effort and energy, had the same qualifications as anybody else, then why shouldn't I expect to get an accounting position just like anybody else?

She tried to argue her point, but I kept saying "Nope."

My perspective has always been that I am not going to short-change myself because of my past. That's when I decided to officially change my major.

Montco was good for me. I spent about a year on the campus finishing up all the classes I needed to get my associate degree. I graduated with honors and pondered whether to go for my four-year degree. Was I going to do all this just to get out of jail? Or was I really going to continue learning to pursue a better life? I was already "out" of jail, since I was in the education-release program and getting closer to being eligible for parole.

"Am I really going to go after something more?" I asked myself.

I put the question to Brother Wazir to get his perspective. I respected his insights, and we discussed my plan every step of the way. I knew he would not bullshit me. He listened. He asked a few questions. "I would go for it," he said.

I started looking into four-year programs.

7

THE GRADUATE

*I*n the summer of 1980, the path to full release took me to a halfway house in North Philadelphia, a few blocks from Temple University. No more racing to and from Graterford State Penitentiary. No more 8 P.M. curfew and the occasional weekend furlough. I was thirty, still a felon serving out my sentence for armed robbery, almost free.

It felt good to be right across town from the Millers in West Philly. Whether I was serving time or serving up turkey on Thanksgiving on Catharine Street, I kept my connection to family. Mom, Lon, all my sisters and brothers lived in my thoughts and in my heart.

On my first day of semifreedom the guy who ran the halfway house greeted me with a set of rules: "You damn well better get back in here by ten o'clock every night," he said. We had to pay minimal rent, about $20 a week. We could leave only for work or school, he said. We had to sign in and out. "Do I have to tell you to stay out of trouble?" he asked.

Nope.

For my whole first week, I came in on time, followed all the curfews, and signed the ledger by the door, but first I had to make it safely to the place. North Philly was rough. The buildings on both sides of the house were boarded up. There was a dive bar or two down the street. Junkies were nodding out on the corners. Garbage piled up in empty lots. I could walk up to Broad Street a block over and see all the way downtown to the statue of William Penn atop City Hall, less than two miles south. But that was a world away. Once upon a time, North Philly was a lovely neighborhood of fine, brick row homes and a lively jazz scene. Then the 1964 race riots ripped up Columbia Avenue, and it still wore the scars when I showed up in the rundown apartment building that served as our halfway house.

One morning I slid into the front seat of my Chevy Nova, turned the key in the ignition—nothing. Dead on the street. I lifted the hood and saw that someone had stolen the battery.

"Happens all the time," the dude in the halfway house told me. "They might try and sell it back to you."

I wished they would. Meanwhile, I replaced the battery, threw a chain over my hood, and locked it down every night.

I had a roommate, but I never saw him. Testing out my newfound freedom, I was sticking by the rules. But I kept wondering: "Where the hell is my roommate?"

One night about a week and a half or so after I showed up, in walked this tall, well-dressed brother.

"Where you been, man?" I asked.

He was an acquaintance from around the way, and jail. He

sat down on the bed he never slept in and gave me the low-down.

"Here's the deal," he said. He had a gravelly voice and tired eyes. Like me, he was working off a felony. "As long as you can tell them that you're working, you pay your rent, and you call them and tell them 'I'm working late,' or 'I'm doing this,' they won't bother you. If you're staying cool and showing up every so often, they will leave you pretty much alone."

I looked him up and down, thinking this was some kind of setup. I questioned him about the ledger that I had been signing and the dude who had warned me about the curfew. He assured me that once I started calling in and didn't cause any trouble, I was all but free.

From that point on, I started doing the same thing he did. I showed up there once a week. I paid my rent. I would call them sometimes and say that I had to work overtime or whatever. Most times it was true, since I was living the life of a working college student, trying to satisfy my professors and making money to afford my meager life, walking a tightrope and occasionally falling off.

I HAD PLENTY of help and guidance making my way from prison to university.

Before I got my associate degree from Montgomery County Community College, Carol and Dick Greenwood made sure I was ready for the next phase. Besides teaching English, part of Greenwood's job was guiding those of us on education release as we progressed toward full release. Dick and I had grown tighter over the years. It's safe to say he was invested in my success.

Once I decided to go for the four-year degree, Greenwood took me around to all the local colleges and universities. We went to Villanova, Penn, Temple, Drexel, and others. Just like a high school senior doing the college tour with his parents, I would walk around the campuses, visit classes, and get applications. Villanova was too small and suburban. Penn was too wealthy and elite. Drexel was focused on engineering. Temple University felt right, and it was willing to accept pretty much all my credits from Montco. The application process was relatively easy, and it had a well-regarded accounting program. I could walk from my halfway house to campus.

The way Carol, Dick Greenwood, and I had worked it out, I would apply to start at Temple as a junior so I could finish up in two years with a bachelor of science degree. Temple would provide the easiest, most convenient, and quickest way for me to get my degree. I applied as a transfer student, Temple accepted me, and with about a year remaining in my sentence, I became a full-time student at a well-regarded four-year university. Temple was known as an inner-city college that, while not an academic rival of Penn, still graduated top-notch professionals.

What were the ingredients of my success at that moment? How did a felon serving time for armed robbery become a college student with his sights set on a degree in accounting—while still serving time?

I can't point to any revelation or breakthrough. I knew I was done with jail and the jail life. Brother Wazir was essential in guiding me through my time inside. He and I would dive into deep discussions about everything from religion to criminal justice to Arabic literature. Islam provided my community and spiritual path. I benefited from Pennsylvania's commitment to giving inmates opportunities to learn and work while serving their sentences.

The desire to change—on the part of the inmate—was an essential ingredient. Sure, I was the same kid who wanted to get a rep on the streets of West Philly. Even as a little boy, once I set my mind to it, I could sell magazines. In college I could master biology and complicated accounting. Once Temple accepted me, and I saw the path to getting a degree and embarking on a career in business, I was all in.

And the more I started to focus on giving this new opportunity my best shot, the more things started to open up for me. For the first time I started to feel the stir of a raw ambition to succeed, together with the confidence that I could pull it off.

AS SOON AS I was settled into the halfway house, I drove across town to Catharine Street. Everyone in my family knew I was out and back in town, and they couldn't wait to reconnect. At least once or twice a week I would take the half hour drive due west across the Schuylkill River—from one oppressed Black neighborhood up against a university to another. North Philly had Temple; West Philly pushed up against the University of Pennsylvania.

Lon and my brothers Jerry and Ted were living in the little

row house on Catharine Street. Lon was still punching the clock at U.S. Gypsum. When I walked into the living room my first Saturday back, the TV was tuned to a Phillies game, Lon was watching from the couch, and Jerry was grabbing a beer from the kitchen.

"C'mon in and settle down," Lon said. My father didn't have to get up and throw his arms around me or anything. He was relieved to see me and proud that I was still pursuing my business degree at Temple. He was cool. I was cool. Phils lost—but they did win the World Series that fall. We all gathered around Lon on Catharine Street to see the home team beat Kansas City.

My sisters had mostly moved on, gotten married, gone to college, and started families. Glo and Leen had graduated from the Community College of Philadelphia, Glo the same year I had gotten my degree from Montco. She was now divorced and raising my nieces in Blackwood, New Jersey.

Mom moved out to a row house a few blocks away on Osage Avenue, farther west and closer to Cobbs Creek Park. She and Lon were not getting along. Catherine's job on the maintenance side at Philadelphia International Airport liberated her. She was good at it, and she'd moved up the ranks to management. She traveled. She needed her own space. I wound up spending more of my time over there, but Catharine Street was still the place where we could always find family and food and sports on TV. My daughter, Laila, lived around the corner and would stop on the way to her favorite candy store. It was always a warm place to be.

The neighborhood itself was not so warm; it was sad, worse, in further decline. In 1970, when I returned from Camp Hill, heroin had hit the neighborhood hard; a decade later it was crack cocaine. People who were solid citizens, holding down jobs and raising children, got hooked. Friends and even family members succumbed to that quick and powerful high. Gang fights over corners were more violent and deadly than ever.

While I had zero interest in drugs—doing them, selling them, or hanging out with people in that world—I refused to cut off old friends who might still walk on the criminal side. A few—like Saleem—had moved on to legal hustles. Cody Blue was still doing his thing. I just wasn't interested in getting caught up in anything that might get me arrested, though I had opportunities and temptations.

I was deeply tied to Islam. No more Mosque No. 12 and the Black Mafia. Everyone from Jabbar to Bo Baynes had been taken down; most were behind bars, if they were still alive. I still showed up at a neighborhood mosque every Friday for Jumma, but the Nation of Islam and all that it meant was in my rear view mirror.

AROUND THIS TIME, Carol and her husband had separated. She and her son, Patren, moved out of their house to a place out in the small town of Blue Bell, close to the Montco campus. After the first few weeks, I rarely went to the halfway house, and ended up unofficially living in Blue Bell with Carol and her son. We started out as friends, and then became more. We got along well, though we didn't have a lot in common. But we were not committed at that point in our relationship. You could say I had commitment problems, and for good reason.

Right before I went to jail this last time, I had gotten married. I had fallen for a girl named Donna. We'd been together for about six months, and we were married for only about two weeks before I went away. But I was in love. She hung in there for a while. Then she ended up having some kids with another guy. So much for love.

When I came home, one of the first things I had to handle was getting a divorce if I was going to try to build my new life. I took a class sponsored by some department of the City of Philadelphia on how to complete your own divorce. I sat through the class, the only man with a big group of women.

Pennsylvania had just started granting no-fault divorces, meaning that if both people agreed on it and there were no children or assets in dispute, you could just sign the document. You then had to wait ninety days, and if nobody contested it after that, the judge would issue the divorce decree. The class showed us how to file all the necessary paperwork, and I filed it all myself. Donna was living somewhere in Jersey, so I went and tracked her down to get her to sign the papers. It was a matter-of-fact meeting, all business. We had both moved on by then.

I got out of Graterford in 1980. The divorce was all settled by 1981.

But the failure and breakup with Donna definitely affected my perspective and my trust level with women. Not that I can blame her for moving on with her life when I got locked up. She was young, and I was gone. But I was hurt, and I was not going to let that happen to me again.

I've tried really hard over the years, but it's been difficult for me to commit to one person. Jail has definitely affected my relationships with women. Over time I had learned how to deal with no women in my life, then I would come home and had to adjust all over again. My jail mentality made it more difficult to build relationships with women, too. They would tell me that I was closed off, and that I didn't share. It was the truth. I might not have wanted to hear that, but I recognize now that it was all too true.

Carol was an exception. She and I grew close over many years. When she was one of my class counselors at Graterford, we were cool, but that was it. I was still in jail. When she became my counselor during the education-release program, we became good friends. Nothing was going on—or so I thought, but I do remember that when I got my grades after my very first semester on Montco's campus, I went right over to Carol's office.

"Check it out," I said and waved the paperwork. "All As!"

That was partly gratitude, since Carol had helped me get acclimated throughout, but I was beginning to feel closer to her.

Carol knew the truth of my predicaments, and we built trust and comfort over time. At a time when I was reaching for opportunities, she made them more available to me. She was the opposite of the women I had dealt with. She was solid, down-to-earth, practical. She was my safe haven in Blue Bell while I was allegedly living at the funky halfway house. About a year later, we were married.

I WAS GOING to school full time at Temple from 8 A.M. to noon. The classes were more challenging than Montgomery County Community College but not overwhelming. Montco had prepared me well for Temple's advanced classes.

I settled in, joined the Black Student Union, and made a few friends on campus. No more dabbling in various subjects. I zeroed in on business development, marketing, and economics. And making a few bucks.

My sister Theresa had hooked me up with a job driving for a limousine company where she was working as a dispatcher. A lot of nights I worked until two or three in the morning. I would drive to New York, Atlantic City, or wherever. So, after a while, I didn't even call the halfway house anymore. They already knew I was still at work. As long as I stayed out of trouble and paid my rent, they didn't bother me. By now, I was either at work, in school, or staying with Carol in Blue Bell.

The hours were too long, though, and it left me little time to study. I was struggling in class. Sometimes I would be up all night working and then go back to Carol's, take a shower, and go straight to school. I was nodding off in class, and it began to affect my grades. Even though the money was good and it was a decent job, I couldn't do both. I had to quit that job, as the stress of being a full-time student and working enough to support myself took its toll. I had trouble paying tuition and rent. I had organized Pell Grants and student loans, but I couldn't get my money right.

If I worked enough to make rent and keep my prison car on the road, I couldn't keep up with the demands of my professors. It all boiled down to the money, as it often does for most folks.

CODY BLUE AND I had been friends since we were kids running around the alleys of West Philly. He saw me go from the smart kid to the Nation member to the stickup artist. He didn't even hold it against me that I had held him up at his club for protection money for the mosque. Cody was a hustler who spread the wealth; we were all in it together.

Knowing Cody was good for a loan, I put word out that I was looking for him. He lived in a modest but large row home with his wife and kids just off Baltimore Avenue. He was a tall, dark-skinned brother whose hair was starting to get a few gray strands. "C'mon in, Larry," he said.

We sat down in his enclosed front porch and got caught up on old friends who were still alive and kicking in West Philly. I explained my current predicament: finishing up my jail term, working to get my college degree across town at Temple.

"I can't make ends meet," I said. "Is there any way you can front me some cash?"

Cody sat back with a grin on his face. He thought I wanted back in the game.

"Look," I said, "this ain't the stuff from before. I'm just asking you to lend me some money so I can finish school. This ain't got nothing to do with that whole other thing. I'm not into that no more. This is a whole different thing."

"Seriously?" he said. Then, "How much you need?"

I don't even remember how much it was now, perhaps seven or eight hundred bucks. I promised to pay him back—with interest. I walked out of Cody's place with enough money to pay my loans and keep my thing going for at least a few more months.

Cody coming through for me was crucial, because the "other thing" could have drawn me right back to the streets. I was that close. Then I got a job, then another job, and I saved money with the full intention of paying Cody back every dime.

When I returned to pay off the loan, Cody was nowhere to be found. Turned out he was murdered one night in a stickup in front of his house. Rather than turn over the cash he always carried, he tried to fight off the robbers. The guy shot him and took all his money. He was cut down before I could pay him back. I had to make it right, so I looked to pay the loan back to his wife.

BROTHER SALEEM, MY old buddy Sonny D, heard I was on the straight and narrow and looking for work. He found me one night on Catharine Street.

"I got something for you," he said. This was the same Saleem who'd been by my side at crucial moments, like joining the Nation and asking Bo Baynes to set us up on the criminal side of Mosque No. 12. Now he was still in West Philly but working the legit side, hustling but without breaking the law. "You want to get paid for working with young people?"

Saleem set me up with an organization that was like Big Brothers Big Sisters. We got paid to spend time with these kids who had been sentenced by the juvenile court to participate in that program. They had gotten into some trouble and had to do this instead of being sent to jail. I could relate, of course, having been in their shoes. Only I went straight to jail, first juvenile, then the real deal. This was my first opportunity to keep young Larry Millers from heading down the prison path, and I got into it.

I was required to spend a certain number of hours per week with each kid who was assigned to me. I scheduled it around my classes, so I might spend all day Saturday hanging out with the kids. We would go to different events and activities, whatever was going on around Philly. I would take them on campus and to the library with me some days.

It was great because I could organize my work schedule around school. I did that for only about a year since I was getting pretty close to graduating, but I found it so rewarding. When it was over, I would look for other opportunities to work with young people. Having gone down the road to prison and then having benefited from people's kindness, I wanted to try to make a difference in young lives, too.

Saleem always had multiple hustles, so he hooked me up with cleaning offices at night. I was doing both jobs, helping the kids and cleaning offices— and studying. The cleaning job worked out well scheduling wise, too. I had a certain area that I was assigned to clean every night. I would get there and just go hard and knock my area out quickly, and then sit in one of the offices and do homework and study.

All of these circumstances seemed to be playing into my being able to finish school and graduate on time.

ONE NIGHT, SALEEM and I went to see Stevie Wonder at the Spectrum. It was a fantastic concert. The weather was freezing cold, and snow was falling when we got to my green, beat-up Chevy Nova. The car sputtered on the way home. Next morning it was dead, totally unfixable. My only way to get around was towed away by noon.

I was back to square one. I had the two jobs, and I had school, but I didn't have a car. I couldn't do it all on public transportation. I was stressing out. And although I was working and had some money coming in, I didn't know how I was going to get a car. I went by Lon's house on Catharine Street, sat down in the kitchen, feeling down, trying to figure out what to do from there. It looked like I was not going to be able to pull off this whole new life, after all.

"Do I have to try to raise some money illegally? Should I step back into the life? What am I gonna do?"

Lon saw the look of defeat on my face.

"What's up? What's the matter wit' you?"

I just shrugged him off and turned away. "I don't want to discuss it," I responded.

Lon had just gotten off his shift at U.S. Gypsum. After some prodding, I explained the whole situation.

"I have money to pay a car note, but I don't have any credit to buy a car."

It wasn't that I had bad credit. I had *no* credit. I had never bought anything on credit in my life.

"So, what do you need?" he asked.

"I need some help to get a car."

"All right. I'll take you up to my boy up on Baltimore Avenue in the morning." His friend had a used car dealership that was very well known in the neighborhood. "Yeah. I'll cosign for you," he said.

"For real? Aww thanks, Lon. You don't even know how much you just helped me."

The next morning, I picked out a red station wagon. Lon co-signed and I made all the payments. I was still driving that red wagon when I landed my first corporate job at Campbell Soup, and one of the first things I did was pay it off completely. Lon had trusted me, and I wanted to make sure that I made good on that. I was all in again, completely recommitted to getting my degree.

Lonnie had pulled me back from the brink.

BUT THE BRINK would still call out to me.

One Saturday afternoon my senior year, I was visiting buddies in West Philly when two of my old crew members with Cedar Avenue cornered me. They wanted to get back into dealing drugs in a major way. They knew that I had been tight with Jabbar in Graterford. Incredibly, Jabbar had gotten out for a time. The Pennsylvania Supreme Court had granted him a new trial for allegedly participating in the Black Mafia's raid on Dubrow's Furniture. My old buddy Seifallah said Jabbar was hanging out in a pool hall up on Germantown Avenue.

"C'mon Larry, set us up with him," they asked.

There was no way I wanted to get back in that business. No way in hell. Yet I felt I owed these brothers, so I agreed to drive up to the pool hall where they said Jabbar had set up shop.

All the way up there, I'm thinking: "What the hell am I getting myself into?"

Sure enough, Nudie Mims and his crew were in the back room

of this pool hall. Last time I had seen Jabbar he was the Imam in control of Graterford. I was still grateful to him for giving me the money to get a car when I was living in the trailers. Now he was looking healthy and strong, as always. We hugged and exchanged greetings.

"*As-salaam alaikum.*"

"What can I do for you brothers?" Jabbar asked.

My two friends expected me to ask, but I was not into it. I have never been half in, half out of anything in my life. I stumbled for words. Everyone could feel it. Jabbar sat there looking at me, perplexed.

Finally, I said: "These two brothers asked me to set up a meeting with you. They have some things to discuss."

And I walked out of the back room, through the pool hall, past the bar, and out onto Germantown Avenue, and left that life in my rearview mirror. Why, I asked myself, had I even put myself in that situation? Suppose I had been set up? Or there were drugs around? Or the cops had busted the place?

I waited outside while my friends worked out whatever they needed from Jabbar. A half hour later they emerged and gave me the thumbs-up.

Jabbar's free time was short-lived. The feds locked him up again and moved him to a penitentiary in Minnesota, where he died in 2012 at the age of sixty-nine.

I AVOIDED THOSE temptations, got through all those hard times, and headed to graduation from Temple University with honors.

The way things worked back then, during your last year of school, several companies would come on campus and recruit students. At that point there was what was referred to as "the Big Eight" accounting firms that every accounting graduate was dying to be recruited by. If you didn't get into one of the Big Eight, then you might as well just cut your wrists—at least that was the way people at Temple viewed things.

I had joined Beta Alpha Psi, the international accounting and financial informational society chapter at Temple. I joined it to make some important connections and maybe pick up some useful information. There was a brother at one of the meetings who worked as a recruiter for one of the Big Eight firms. People were buzzing all around him and trying to get an edge. I waited and played the back. When he broke free, I cornered him.

I said: "Look, I need you to tell me something. What is it that you look for in an interview when you're recruiting somebody? What kinds of answers are you listening for?"

We stood there and talked for about an hour, and he laid out exactly what he looked for, what kinds of questions he asked and wanted to hear, what types of answers he hated hearing from candidates. He was just putting it all out for me. I was thinking, "This is great!"

"What's the one thing you look for from a candidate?" I asked.

"Confidence," he said. He wanted to see that a candidate was going to bring that with them if hired.

I filed that away and took it one step further. I decided to do some interviews with companies that I didn't want to work for. No matter what, if they offered me the job, I was not going to work for them. But I set all those interviews up first so that I could practice. By the time the Big Eight accounting firms came onto campus, I was locked and loaded, so to speak.

One of the questions that showed up in most interviews was the typical: "So, where do you see yourself in five years?"

When I was doing the practice interviews, I was always trying to figure out the right answer to that question. Not only what is the correct answer they want to hear, but what do I really want to do?

Even though my focus was on finance, that didn't necessarily mean I wanted to be a controller or CFO or a partner at a public accounting firm. The more I thought about it, the answer I came up with was that in five years I saw myself in a position where I'd help to make decisions that would determine the company's direction, as opposed to being somebody who carried out the decisions that had already been made by others.

"I want to be a decision-maker," I said. "I'm willing to take on the responsibility of whether the decisions are good ones. If I make good decisions, great. If I make bad decisions, I'd take responsibility for those, too—and move on."

Interviewers loved that.

I believed it. I didn't want to pigeonhole myself and say that I wanted to be a finance person. If that was what it was, or what it turned out to be, then fine. But if I could go beyond that, I believed it was worth the shot.

I ended up getting offers from seven of the eight companies. But I was a little bit nervous about going into public accounting, since I had felonies.

At this point, nobody at Temple or the firms where I was interviewing knew anything about my past.

AS I'VE SAID before, I pursued Arthur Andersen.

I had really liked the people who'd been interviewing me. The whole process had been going well, and I felt good about my prospects for moving up quickly inside the firm. I connected with the partner who served as their key recruiter. Like most of the top executives, he was a white dude who showed up in a crisp, white shirt, tie tightly knotted to the collar, wing tips. But during the interviews, we were trading stories and laughing with one another.

So, I let my guard down and rolled the dice. He was the one I decided could handle the truth: that I had served time. It was a huge gamble, but I decided to tell him and see what happened. I had already gone through a series of interviews; he was the last before the job offer.

"Look," I said, "I've got to tell you something." And I laid it all out for him. I told him that I really liked who they were as a company, and that I wanted to be straight with them and let them know my story. I told him everything, and I watched his face deflate.

"Wow. I am so proud of you for what you've been able to accomplish," he said. "I so appreciate the fact that you shared this with me."

He reached into his jacket and said: "I have an offer letter here to give to you, but I can't do it. I can't take a chance on one of our clients coming back to me with this if something were to happen down the line."

I told him that I got it, I understood. We shook hands, and I never saw the dude—or the inside of Arthur Andersen—again.

TWO THINGS EMERGED from that moment of full disclosure: First, I never mentioned my felonies again, ever, in my business life. Second, I switched from interviewing at public accounting firms. I had plenty of options. Campbell Soup, based across the Delaware River in Camden, New Jersey, was looking for accountants at the time. I landed a position in their management trainee program. My advisor in Temple's accounting program was surprised. He knew I had been interviewing with major accounting firms and had advocated for me. He stopped me a few days before graduation.

"So, Larry, how come you took a job with Campbell's rather than one of the accounting firms?" he asked. "I know you got some offers."

"True," I responded, "but it turns out the Campbell's offer would give me more options on the business side."

"I don't understand," he said. "Accounting is your strength."

What he didn't understand was that my felonies would always stand in the way of a career in public accounting. I wasn't about to explain that wrinkle. The secret began to take form.

Campbell's turned out to be a great job. My starting salary was $16,500. That was a big deal. I felt rich.

How did I get around my criminal past? The application

asked whether I had been convicted of a crime in the past five years. I checked "NO." Because it was true. It didn't ask if I had *ever* "served time" or been charged with any crimes. I filled out the form accurately, and from that day on, I never had to deal with another employment application. I survived on my résumé.

I loved Campbell's, and I really loved that job. It launched me.

On the job I also clammed up about my past. I severed it from my present. I appreciate the guys I met at Campbell's. We worked hard and had a blast. I made lasting friendships there. Not one person knew about my life on the streets or behind bars.

I kept the secret inside. It wasn't easy, especially when I slept.

Two weeks into the Campbell's gig I woke up in a cold sweat. I dreamt I was walking toward my car after work when a cop car screeched to the curb, two officers jumped out, cuffed me, and threw me in the back.

"Where are you taking me?" I asked. "This must be a mistake!"

"No mistake," the driver said. "You're going back to jail."

It was the first of many crippling dreams. The higher I rose, the greater the stakes, the more troubling the nightmares.

8

THE CLIMB

A year or so into my first job at Campbell Soup I got a call from my buddy Vince Melchiorre.

"How come you didn't take this job we had for you over here at Mrs. Paul's?" he asked.

Vince and I had gotten to be very tight—a South Philly Italian and a brother from West Philly in it together. We had joined Campbell's trainee program at the same time. He and I had bonded in part because we were the only ones who didn't need a connection, family or otherwise, to get into the program. We'd gotten hired strictly on merit.

"What job?" I asked.

Vince had already moved over to Mrs. Paul's, a subsidiary of Campbell's that produced frozen fish. At Campbell's we used to go sit in his car on our lunch breaks and listen to Eddie Murphy tapes and die laughing in the parking lot. He would come out to my house for dinner with the family. He would tell me stories about his grandmother who still lived down in South Philly, and her naïve view of some of the guys from their old neighborhood. She'd be like, "Oh, Little Nicky? He's such a nice, good boy."

Vince would tell her, "Little Nicky is a gangster, Grandmom! Stay away from him, he kills people!"

As soon as Vince got settled in Mrs. Paul's he started looking out for me.

"My boss called over there and he had a job for you here. He was told that you weren't interested."

"What are you talking about?" I asked.

"Things are cranking over here, and we need you. Crazy you didn't know about this," Vince said. "You need to find out what happened."

Things were bubbling all over Philly at the time. Besides being an enthusiastic sports town and the "cradle of liberty" with Independence Hall and the Liberty Bell, Philadelphia and the region was loaded with manufacturing plants, from the refineries along the Schuylkill River to plants that produced Tastykake snacks, Campbell's Soup, and Breyers ice cream.

It occurred to me that my bosses at Campbell's had blocked me, big time. Granted, I was hardly a heavyweight; at that moment I was still in training. But every opportunity could be crucial in the corporate world, and too many people allow themselves and their careers to be controlled. I at least wanted to have the option to take the new job, even if I didn't want it.

I had two choices: go along and let it pass, or confront the guys who were in the position to block me. Both were middle-aged white guys, assistant controllers who had been with Campbell's for years. The senior guy looked like he walked right out of a Klan meeting: buzzed haircut, pudgy, humorless, mean. Right after Vince called, I went to their joint offices.

"I understand that there was some interest in me for a position over at Mrs. Paul's," I said. "I also understand that they were told that I wasn't interested."

Sure, it was a risky move, but I was not afraid. On the outside I was oxford shirt and tie. But on inside I was still . . . me.

They looked at one another. The senior guy fixed me with a level stare and nodded.

"I really don't appreciate the fact that I wasn't even talked to or asked about that opportunity," I said.

"Well, uh, well," he said. His voice trailed off. "We thought that it was what was best for your career . . ."

"You know what?" I responded. "I appreciate that, but let me be involved in deciding what's best for my career. Whether I would want to take the job or not, I feel like I should have had the option to decide. It shouldn't have been that a decision was made without me even knowing about it. I at least should have had the opportunity to say: 'Yes, I'm interested' or 'No, thank you.'"

He didn't apologize, but he did say: "You're right, you're right."

"I understand the position is still open, and I plan to interview for the job," I said.

They were not pleased, but they knew they were wrong.

Stone-faced, I walked out and called Vince. He'd already told me that they still had not filled the position. I interviewed with Vince's boss at Mrs. Paul's. He said that I impressed him by talking about concepts of accounting rather than simply keeping books. Since I would be coming from Campbell's, he did not require a formal job application. No questions about my past, other than my Temple degree.

My new gig: supervisor for cost accounting at Mrs. Paul's.

A few months later I met Vince's grandmother at his wedding.

"You look like such a nice, good boy," she said.

Also, a gangster, when necessary.

AFTER THE FIRST year of my career in corporate management, I realized I had a natural instinct for when to push through obstacles and when to hold back. I also realized my understanding of basic accounting and business economics was strong, thanks to my studies. From the streets I had developed a B.S. meter to distinguish people I could trust. And I worked my ass off.

What, I asked myself, could hold me back? How could I make sure I was qualified for every promotion? How could I make certain that I wasn't being held back for being Black? I understood that race, whether or not it's stated or acknowledged, is typically a factor when decisions are made in the corporate world.

After work I discussed it with Vince. Being a white guy, he had a hard time seeing it, but he could understand why my being Black might have been one reason the two guys at Campbell's had not told me about the job offer.

"If the color of my skin is the reason for denying me a better job," I explained, "I want to clear away any other reasons, so everyone can see it is based solely on race."

In my crusade to break down any obstacle that might appear, I zeroed in on the last piece of my education. I needed a master's degree in business administration. Campbell's offered to pay full tuition reimbursement for their employees, but getting an MBA was the last thing I had time for. Carol and I had two children together, Jamal and Amissa. I was commuting to Camden from our place in Norristown and working about sixty hours a week. The idea of taking classes at night and studying all weekend was not appealing. Quite honestly, it was the absolute last thing I wanted to do.

Still, at some point soon I would be up for a job, and I would be qualified, but I would be competing with somebody who had an MBA. I chose La Salle because it had a part-time program, and I went on evenings and weekends for two and a half years.

I graduated from La Salle with my MBA. There—I had the letters after my name, one less hurdle against promoting me

I also knew how to play the game, if playing well was working hard and taking advantage of opportunities. At Campbell's corporate office, they'd asked for volunteers to work on a Quality of Work Life Committee. I jumped at it. It gave me the opportunity to meet colleagues from across the company—executives and truckers, machinists and quality control folks, the tasters. We met and talked about how work fit into our lives away from the plant, or kids and our commutes, basic stuff. I made friends along the way, but it also was strategic: those connections could lead to future advantages and opportunities.

Even so, there were no guarantees for success in the corporate world, just as there was no guarantee of survival on the streets or in prison. But I was quietly determined, right from the start.

CAMDEN, NEW JERSEY, is a small, gritty city right across the Delaware River from Philly. The civil rights struggle of the 1960s had hollowed out the center of the city, but manufacturing plants still hugged the river, where Campbell's main soup production facility was located. When a job opened up there for the accounting manager, the department heads came over to Mrs. Paul's and interviewed me for the job, then offered me the position. No application necessary; no résumé required. The secret survived another job change.

My first week on the job I walked into the daily morning meeting where the plant manager met with his department heads.

"Man, Bobby, what the fuck were you doing yesterday afternoon?" was the way he opened the meeting. "You nearly broke down the whole damn supply chain."

"I didn't blow that," the guy shot back. He pointed to another department head. "Ask his sorry ass what happened."

My eyes must have gone wide, and I was wondering if they were going to start swinging.

"Siddown!" the plant manager yelled. Then they started sorting out why the production line had problems the day before.

What had I gotten myself into? They were all up in this meeting yelling, arguing, and cursing each other out for at least a half hour. Red-faced, waving their arms, and pointing fingers and dropping f-bombs all over the room. Everyone was a "motherfucker."

When it was over, they got up and laughed and talked about the "fuckin' Phils." "Who's ready for a cup of coffee?" the plant manager asked. "Come on, let's go." He saw me standing in the back and came up to shake my hand. "Enjoy your first meeting?"

Not really, but I did learn an essential lesson baked into their workdays. They talked to each other directly, roughly, no bull-shit. For these guys, that type of interaction was not personal. It was about somebody who didn't do their job. It had nothing to do with someone liking or not liking someone else as a person. Their MO was: I still like you, and we're still cool. We'll still hang out this weekend and BBQ, but I'm gonna let you know that you didn't do your job.

You don't typically see that in corporate America. So, it was kind of refreshing. People tend to take it personally if you jump on their case about something, but these guys never did.

Every day was a new day. They would have a goal to produce a certain amount of product. If they hit their goal, then that was great. If they didn't, then they knew they had to make up for it the next day, and that was that. The drill was: "Okay, we screwed up yesterday, we can make it up tomorrow," because we were just making soup. Or SpaghettiOs, or Franco-American spaghetti with meatballs.

The Camden job was actually one of my favorite gigs. The guys left it all in the plant. Me, too.

By 1991, Carol, our two kids, her son, Patren, and I were living in Harleysville, a small suburban community about thirty miles north of Philly. I had climbed relentlessly up through midlevel corporate gigs at Campbell Soup to assistant controller at Philadelphia Newspapers Inc. (which later became Greater Philadelphia Newspaper Group) to my latest: manager of general accounting for the dairy division at Kraft Foods in Cherry Hill, New Jersey. I successfully managed the books for the entire division that produced everything from Velveeta cheese to Breyers and Sealtest ice cream. I took every opportunity to visit the ice cream plant at Gray's Ferry so I could sample ice cream right off the line. Not a bad perk!

THE DRIVE FROM Harleysville through Philly and across the Delaware River was more than an hour back and forth every day. Cell phones weren't common back then, so I listened to a lot of talk radio and books on tape to help the time pass and to help me decompress from the day. I would listen to tapes of Warith Deen Mohammed's speeches, sports on the radio, and lots of jazz. The commute gave me a chance to get into the right mindset before going to work, and then to chill out from the day on my way home from work. The transitional time was good for me.

It was also a good time to swing through West Philly and visit everyone in the hood. Most of the family was still in the area. Laila still lived nearby with her mother and her family. I would take Laila out for dinner, I would stop by to check on Mom, or Lon and I would eat takeout and watch TV. My sisters joined in on special occasions. We stayed tight. I did my best to stay close with old buddies as well.

One day I saw Saleem sitting on a stoop on Fifty-Second Street by Malcolm X Park. From the time we first started to hang out together as kids, Sonny D was someone I looked up to, a model in many ways. He was a couple of years older, taller, and always clean: slacks creased, shoes shined, often a fedora.

Today, though, he wasn't looking too good. His head hung over a rumpled shirt.

Sonny D and I were tight for good reason. We had been in Camp Hill together, me for the homicide, Sonny D for assault. We joined the Nation together, when he became Saleem. While I was in Graterford, Saleem went straight and became a small businessman. He was a kind of consultant or contractor, meaning he always had a hustle. He hooked me up with gigs while I was getting my degree at Temple. It's safe to say Saleem played a crucial role in important parts of my life.

I pulled over, got out, and walked over to talk, but my best buddy was nodding out. I could tell he was high on heroin.

"Man, Saleem, what the fuck are you doing that for again?" I asked. "You can do so much better."

Heroin had been Saleem's problem for a long time. And for a long time, I did my best to help him break the habit. I tried to talk him into therapy. He would be clean for months, then he would fall back into it. I cannot recall how many times I saw Saleem out of it. "Get it together!" I would yell at him. And he would promise to get clean. And he would relapse. What was hard for Saleem's family and friends was that he was so smart and savvy and together most of the time, making deals and making money—and helping me get through college.

I walked him to the corner to get a cup of coffee. "I'm okay," he said.

I pointed the car north and headed out of town back to Harleysville, but Saleem was not okay. A few months later a friend called to tell me that Saleem was dead. He'd gotten into a scuffle, and the guy pulled out a knife and killed my friend. I drove right down to Cobbs Creek to be with his mother and his wife and kids. To this day we stay close, and to this day I miss my man, Sonny D.

What I didn't miss was the inner turmoil I suffered thanks to my secret. Every promotion brought more responsibility and, potentially, more scrutiny. Frankly, I cannot explain how I managed to keep my criminal life and time served behind bars out of my business career. And frankly, I never rested easy, knowing that my past could show up any day and take a lead pipe to my career.

Acel Moore knew. The legendary journalist and I got to be friends when I worked in finance for Philadelphia Newspapers, Inc., the company that owned the *Philadelphia Inquirer* and the *Daily News*. Moore was a groundbreaking Black journalist. He rose from reporter to editor to columnist at the *Inquirer* and encouraged young African Americans to join newsrooms, not just in Philly but around the country. He demanded newspapers cover Black communities. One of his allies and sources was Bennie Swans, a West Philly brother who'd survived Vietnam and came home to advocate for his community by starting Safe Streets, Inc.

Bennie had joined me as a member of the Cedar Avenue gang. We ran together, drank together, fought other gangs together.

One day Acel took the elevator up from the newsroom to the business floor and strolled over to my desk. He said he was reporting out a column about some lasting feuds in Cobbs Creek. Said he'd spoken to Bennie, and Bennie suggested he might want to check with me.

"Can you tell me a little about this?" he asked. He gave me that look that he knew, maybe not my whole backstory, but enough. I'm not sure I was much help on his column, but I also knew my secret was safe with him. And he never told.

Still, it was another reminder that my fear of being found out was justified. I lived in perpetual fear. The higher I rose, the greater the stakes. At night, the nightmares grew more vivid and frightening.

The tap on the shoulder. The cop throwing me in the patrol car. The judge ordering me to prison. The CO slamming the bars of my cell.

"NO!" I would scream. "This is a mistake."

MY OTHER REGULAR stop along the commute home brought me back to jail—in real life. I could hook a left on Route 73 off the main highway and be at Graterford State Penitentiary in less than twenty minutes. I would give Brother Wazir a heads-up, and we would meet up in the trailers outside of the wall.

More often I would visit on weekends and take the two younger kids. There was a makeshift playground by the trailers for visiting families, and there were vending machines with all manner of chips and candy. One Sunday my son, Jamal, then about four, got into the car for the drive home, gave me a puzzled look, and asked: "What is this place?"

For him and Amissa, it was a kind of playdate. For me it was a part of my life I never wanted to leave behind, let alone forget.

Brother Wazir and I could still sit and talk for hours, debating Islam and the finer points of the Qur'an. He and I were about the same age, though his hair was starting to salt-and-pepper long before mine. Wazir never ceased to impress me with his energy and inquisitiveness. He'd learned Arabic and Spanish. He was teaching other inmates. He maintained his connection to his three daughters. And he was all but running the farm attached to Graterford, raising vegetables and beef. Meantime, he was building his case for commutation and appealing it up to the governor.

"I'm close to getting out," he told me one Sunday afternoon in 1988.

He'd been serving time for murder since 1968. Ironically, his three accomplices had gotten out. Two had testified for the state and served one year each; one had served five years and gotten out on retrial when the accomplices refused to testify against him. That left Wazir behind bars serving life. Wazir had started seeking commutation in 1979 but was denied public hearings. Starting in 1983, his case had gone before the Board of Pardons, whose members had recommended his reduction in sentence—for the third time. Each time the governor had declined. Now he was in the governor's hands again.

When I came back a few weeks later, Brother Wazir delivered the bad news: "The governor refused."

That would happen four more times. Then commutation hearings would be denied. Wazir kept at it—and so did I; through visits to Graterford and in work behind the scenes, I made Wazir's release part of my personal mission. I would wage a quiet campaign until Wazir was out—whatever it took.

MY FIRST STOP every Thursday morning on my way to work was a middle school in a rough part of North Philly on Germantown Avenue, not far from Temple University.

On a typical morning the principal would get on the loudspeaker and say; "Good morning and congratulations. There were no fights on school grounds yesterday. Thanks to everyone."

Teaching a class in money management to the middle school students was part of my volunteer work with Junior Achievement. These were kids like me, but in a different part of my hometown. The school was in bad shape. Windows were dirty and barred. The neighborhood was worse: boarded-up row homes, check-cashing joints, drunks and junkies and crackheads all over.

But for me, the school was one of the few places during the week where I felt centered, where my disparate lives felt as if they could come together. Maybe there was a Larry Miller in the class, a kid with a good head and determination to work hard and make a success out of a life from rough beginnings.

Maybe I could reach that kid. I would always try.

IN 1992, I found myself back in Holmesburg Prison, the decaying jail in northeast Philly. This was no nightmare.

"Look around you," a man in a sharp suit and tie said. "Prisoners have been jailed here since 1896." He swept his hand down the row of cells that still held inmates. "Prison reform is an essential movement for us."

I looked down the cellblock to see if I could remember which one had held me, when I made the brief stop here before Camp Hill. I also wondered whether one of the guards would stop and give me that look and ask: "Didn't you serve time here?"

At the moment I was serving time with the Philadelphia Urban League Leadership Institute. It was a networking and community education program for up-and-coming African Americans taking leadership roles in business, government, nonprofits, community, or media. My colleagues at Kraft had nominated me to participate.

Standing there, I did have an urge to say, "I was once one of the prisoners here," but the urge quickly passed. Instead, I listened closely and kept my mouth shut for the entire tour. I had to think long and hard before even attending the event.

The fifty or sixty participants in our Leadership Institute group met once a month for tours of Harrisburg and various conferences as well as a capstone, which was a competitive research project. We divided up into groups, each group selected a topic and produced a paper, and a panel of judges from the Urban League graded each to come up with the prizewinner. My group selected: "The Survival of the Black Male."

We dug into the subject. I brought some relevant—real-life, so to speak—experiences and perspective. But I chose not to delve into the details of how I had survived the streets, made it through two terms in prison, benefited from education release, and climbed the corporate ladder to qualify for a leadership program. I had buried my secret too deeply in my past. There was no way I would discuss my felonies in this setting, with this group, as I was rising through my career.

Did we solve the multifaceted problem? No. But we did write a report that spelled out systemic problems for Black men and recommended specific improvements to public education and job training. We included a section about prison-release programs for work and education. I added a few essentials from my playbook: stand up for yourself, don't settle, pick your battles, be confident, work hard. I relied on my personal experience to guide the research and help write the report. And we won the prize for the top project.

The year after we won, I was invited to the next class's graduation ceremony as an alumnus. My boss at Kraft, Vicki, had sponsored somebody in the program that year, and she and I ended up going to the graduation ceremony together. We went into the ballroom where the event was being held. Since it's the Urban League, it was about 90 percent Black folks in the house. I knew a bunch of people there, and she and I mingled around and worked the room. As we were leaving, she pulled me aside.

"I need to tell you something," she said. "Being one of only a few white people in a whole room of Black people made me feel a bit uncomfortable.

"You know," she continued, "now I know how you must feel every day."

I didn't know how to respond. Clearly it was something she had to get off her chest. She was right: at Kraft and at Mrs. Paul's and at Campbell Soup, for that matter, I was often the only African American in the room or at the table. That was my life.

I looked Vicki in the eye and said, "Thanks. I appreciate you even recognizing that, and for being willing to share that with me. You're absolutely right. This is something that me and most Black people in corporate America have to deal with every day. Going in to work and feeling that level of discomfort because you're one of two, or one of one."

THE MIGRAINES STARTED when I was working for Campbell Soup and we were living in Harleysville.

They would come at me without warning, any time, day or night. I had rarely suffered from headaches in my life. Now I was experiencing brutal pain behind my forehead and a pounding at the top of my head. They would bring me to my knees and send me into dark rooms.

One particularly brutal migraine forced me to the emergency room. Doctors and nurses took care of the pain but recommended a bunch of tests. I came back for spinal taps and neurological examinations.

"Every test came back negative," the doctor reported. "Everything's normal."

Not quite.

These sudden migraines were caused by my anxiety over the secret getting out. It was the cost of living two lives. Every day I had to separate the gangster from the accountant. It was always present in my mind. It was a miracle that the secret had survived for more than a decade. I paid in migraines. My secret and its effects remained the same, even as I evolved. The longer I stayed in Philly, the greater the risk of it getting out.

I WAS STEWING over the secret one day at work when the phone rang with a call from a former colleague. "Hey, Larry, my new outfit has some openings that might fit your skills," he said. He had left Kraft to work for VF Corporation, a global apparel company based in Reading. It had started in 1899 as Schuylkill Silk Manufacturing, became Vanity Fair Silk Mills, then shortened down to VF Corporation. It owned Lee Jeans, Wrangler, JanSport, Jantzen, and a few other brands. Currently they own Vans, Timberland, and Supreme, just to name a few. "We need a controller for Lee Jeans in Kansas City or Jantzen in Portland."

The next week I drove seventy miles northwest to Reading, a small city that happened to be a mecca for outlet malls. The executives and I hit it off. They were impressed with my experience and success at Kraft. If I could manage the business affairs for plants that turned out Sealtest ice cream, sports apparel would be a piece of cake. They flew me out to Kansas City to interview with Lee and then to Portland to interview with Jantzen.

Kansas City was okay, but Portland in August was captivating. The light, the temperature, the vibe—kind of mesmerizing. At the time, all I knew about Portland was that it was where the NBA's Trail Blazers played. They were the only reason that I knew Portland existed. I knew Nike was there, too.

Back at VF in Reading, I got called into a meeting with Jerry Johnson, the chief financial officer. I guess that made him number two in the executive hierarchy.

"Well," he said, "turns out they both want to offer you the controller position. Which do you prefer?"

Johnson was a white guy in his midfifties, easygoing, competent, and down-to-earth, literally. He and his wife lived on a farm nearby. He rarely showed up wearing a tie.

"Not sure," I said. "What do you think?"

I had a sense right off the bat that this guy and I were going to be good for one another. He fed off my confidence; I appreciated his taking the time to hear me out—and tell me what he thought, which I knew was coming.

"Jantzen," he said. "Better situation for you. I can see you doing well out there. They need your skills."

"Done," I said. "When do I start?"

With that, Jerry Johnson became my mentor inside VF and beyond. It might seem a bit strange to compare him to Brother Wazir, but both became central guides at crucial times in my life. Just in different situations.

Before I met with Jerry, I had studied Jantzen. It was like the Nike of its time—fifteen or twenty years before I started working there. It was one of the first companies in the sports apparel world to use athletes and celebrity endorsers. From a marketing and advertising perspective, a lot of the things that had contributed to Nike's success Jantzen had already been doing for a long time. Jantzen was a $200 million company when that was a ton of value. But it never grew beyond being a $200 million company. They just kinda got stuck.

By the time I got to Jantzen the company was struggling and stagnant. Nike had blown right by them. They didn't move forward with the times. They lost the vision of how to continue to grow and how to stay relevant from a consumer perspective. And that was where Nike was always successful. They understood how to market and how to stay relevant. They had a vision for where they wanted to take the company. That was a major difference between the two. The question was whether I could help bring Jantzen back into the game.

WHEN I DROVE myself cross-country to Portland in September 1992, Lon was sick. He'd been in and out of the hospital with throat cancer. After I left, he had gone back into the hospital.

I moved into a small apartment the company had gotten for me that was right across the street from the office. Until Carol and the kids came out, my plan was to go back and forth to Philly once a month.

I had been in Portland for two weeks when Jerry Johnson and

a couple of the senior corporate people flew their private plane out from Reading. I was settling into the job well. I knew the drill and quickly got a handle on the business end. Jerry was pleased. He asked when I was going back to Philly. I told him that I had a ticket to return the next week.

"I think you should go back with us," he said.

I told him no thanks, and that I was fine waiting. Again, he said that I should fly back home with them, and again I told him that I was good with my ticket and my plan to go home the following week. We went back and forth a few times.

"You're going with us," he said. "You need to go home. You need to see your family. That's it."

He didn't know that my father was sick or anything that I had going on in Philly. "All right, man," I said. "Damn."

So, I jetted home on their brand-new Falcon 900. This trip was the first time they had ever used it and my first time in a private jet. They had a rental car waiting for me when we got to Reading, and I drove home.

The next day I went up to the hospital and I hung out with Lon. I helped cut his toenails for him and stuff like that, just spent the whole day with him. That next day, Saturday, Mom came by. Though she had moved out, they had never divorced. My sister Glo, Carol, Jamal, Amissa, and I were all up at the hospital hanging out with him and having a good time. He was in good spirits. We were laughing and joking, just enjoying being together. At one point, Lon reached across his chest, undid his watch, and handed it to me. Without saying a word, I put it on my wrist. The room was quiet.

"Looks good on you," Lon said.

By the time we had driven from the hospital in West Philly back home to West Oak Lane, Mom called. "Lon has passed," she said.

A lot of things went through my mind, of course, but overall I was happy that I had had the time with Lon. If I had waited in Portland until the following week and come home when I'd planned to, I would have missed that opportunity to be there and spend that time with him. Things like that happen for a reason. I was supposed to be there in Philly.

That's the thing. Sometimes, whatever you believe the higher power is, whether you call it God, Allah, the universe, or whatever, it sends us messages and gives insights—if we listen. I think a lot of times we don't. I've had a number of situations throughout my life where someone has looked out for me, or something that wasn't supposed to happen happened, or, vice versa, something that was supposed to happen didn't. There is a force or a power that has always led me to do things that have worked out to my benefit, even when I didn't want to do them. We often get signs, messages, things that are trying to guide us on our path, and we should listen. I call it being blessed.

A few days later we held a memorial for Lon at Brown and Hill Funeral Home on Fifty-Eighth and Arch Streets. It was jammed with friends and family. Lon's coworkers and buddies from U.S. Gypsum showed. Laila came back from her freshman semester at Howard University in Washington, D.C.

Looking out on all of Lon's people, I felt the need to say something. Lon was not a church-going type. The preacher really didn't know my father. So, at a certain point I walked up to the podium. It was one of the hardest things I ever had to face. All the emotions—the sadness, the gratitude, the regrets—welled up in my gut. I started to talk about my dad but broke down.

It was the first time many in my family had ever seen me cry.

BRIAN EPSTEIN, WHO ran Jantzen's swimwear division, called me over for a cup of coffee one day. I had been at Jantzen for maybe six months.

"Instead of being in this controller job, you should come over and help me run swimwear," he said.

Brian and I had gotten to be pretty tight in a short time. We were very cool.

"How would that work?" I asked.

Jantzen had a few divisions at the time, but women's swimwear was their top seller. Brian said that he could really use the help and I could learn a lot more about the business. He was strong with respect to marketing and sales. He had a great eye for product. He could get up in front of a group and sell it. But when it came to tracking the numbers, focusing on the bottom line, and generating margins and all that, he needed some help. He assured me he could work out the details.

"I'm up for that, Brian," I said, "if you help me learn the other parts of this stuff that you know." Like marketing and selling.

"Works for me," he said. "It's a deal."

We pitched that to the president, and he went along with it. Brian and I were now running the swimwear division. My new role was director of business development for women's swimwear. Once we started working together, business was just on fire from then on. We completely revamped marketing, sales, and branding. Revenues began to rise.

A year or so after that, a guy who had worked at Jantzen left for another company, then came to me and offered me a job. I went to the folks at Jantzen and said: "Look, I got this job offer. I don't wanna leave, but unless . . ." and they stepped up and promoted me to vice president of business development for the whole company. About six months into that position, another opportunity emerged.

Every quarter, Jantzen's president, Jay Titsworth, and I would go to VF's corporate headquarters to have our regular business reviews. It was all the "Here's what we did" and "Here's where we're going" presentations. In my role as vice president in control of business development and marketing, I backed up Titsworth.

In late 1993, I had taken a red-eye from Portland back to Philly for the quarterly meeting in Reading. The whole night before, I couldn't get any sleep. I kept having these crazy thoughts about running the company. I didn't know where that was coming from. Maybe it was from some of the questions that Jerry Johnson and some of the other corporate leaders had been asking me about Titsworth, the company, and the business that typically wouldn't be directed at me. There was a sense within Jantzen that Titsworth was on his way out. Something just felt strange.

We got into town and were all set to give our presentation

the next day. Jerry and the CEO and all the other people in the meeting were directing all their questions to me, even though Jay Titsworth was at the table. I was dealing with it and handling the questions, but all the time I was thinking: "Why are they asking me when this dude is sitting right here?"

When we were done, I headed back to my room. The phone rang, and it was Jerry Johnson.

"When are you planning to go back to Portland?" he asked.

I told him that I was on a flight out the next morning.

"Can you change that?" he asked. "Let me tell you why. Jay's out. We've decided we want you to take over out there."

I was speechless.

"Why don't you come in to headquarters tomorrow morning so that we can work out the details?" he asked. "I will be right there with you to work through all of it."

This would be my first time running a company. My head hit the pillow that night and I thought, "I'm prepared to be at the top, seeing as I had started at the bottom." It began with accounting, balancing the books—the basics. At every move up from general accounting to business development to marketing, I had learned how to manage people, delegate when possible, and make hard decisions when necessary. I was ready to step into the new role and run the company.

The next day, Jerry and I sat down and planned how the transition was going to happen.

"This is great, and I can handle this," I said, "but it would make a major difference if you came out to Portland and made the announcement to everybody. It would show that corporate has given me their blessing." I didn't want to return to Portland and suddenly start telling people what to do.

He said, "You know, that's a good idea." We talked it out, and we flew back to Portland the next day. We set up a meeting with the leadership team and made the announcement.

NO PROBLEM. EXCEPT for one.

There was one guy who . . . I just knew he wasn't feeling it. I could tell by the look on his face and his vibe. He was kind of new there, but he was one of these guys who came in with the expectation that at some point he'd be running the company. He was thrown off by this sudden change.

So, after Jerry announced my move up, I went straight down to his office. "Look," I said, "it seems like you have a problem with this."

He said: "No, I don't have a problem with it, but, you know, I just think it would have been nice if they had given an opportunity for other people to apply for it or at least throw their names in the hat. I would have liked to, but, you know, that was their call."

"So, you're not going to have a problem with this?"

He said, "No, no! I'm good. We can work together, there's no problem."

"Cool."

About a week or two later, I set up an off-site event for the key staff members at this place called Skamania Lodge, which is out by the Columbia River Gorge, about forty-five minutes out from Portland. The goal of the event was to set strategies for the company and decide what our key objectives were going to be in order to drive the company where it needed to go. I've always believed that the leadership team has to be aligned on those strategic priorities. Otherwise, you're not going to be successful. It should get to a point where even if you don't necessarily agree 100 percent, everyone will still support the decisions.

Like: "Hey, this might not be the way I would do it, but if this is what the team thinks is the right thing, or if this is what the leader is saying we need to do, then I've got to get behind it." And I was the new leader.

The first day was just a total waste. Every time we thought we were going to be able to get something done, the one guy who had the problem with me taking over would create a disruption. We made no progress. That night we were all having dinner together at the restaurant in the lodge. After dinner, he left and went up to his room. I sat there and listened as the team all started tearing him apart. I mean, they were killing him. The verdict: "He's holding us back!"

I took it all in and said: "We're all supposed to meet at eight tomorrow morning, but you guys, don't come down until nine o'clock. By the time you come down, he'll be gone."

I asked the human resources executive to meet me for breakfast the following morning at eight. Then I had to call Jerry Johnson, since this guy had been hired by the corporate folks.

"Look," I said, "here's what I got for you . . ." and I explained the whole thing.

"Uh, all right, Miller," he said. "I'll cover for you. I got it. I'm gonna take the ass-kickin' for you on this end."

"I appreciate that, Jerry, but I gotta do this."

The next morning at eight, the HR representative and I were waiting for him when he showed up. The three of us had the place to ourselves.

"This just isn't working out for us," I said. "I really don't think it's a good fit for you, either. I believe it would be best for everyone if you would find a more suitable place to better utilize your skills."

He stared at us. He looked around. He understood. Happy? Not quite. Resigned? Indeed.

There were a couple of reasons why I had to do that. The first was that I had to show the team that I was leading the company, and that I was willing to make the tough calls when they needed to be made. Also, they needed to know that if one of them decided to behave the same way, they would be next. Had I not let him go, I would not have had the respect of the rest of the team. I would not have been able to move things forward.

He left that morning. The rest of the team came down at nine.

"He's gone," I said. "Now let's get to work."

We started cranking after that. We ended up having a great off-site meeting, working on strategies and plans for the future of the company. Had I not forced the dude out, he would have held us all back and made everybody look bad—especially me.

A YEAR INTO my running Jantzen, all of the numbers across our divisions were up. We were selling more apparel, broadening our markets, increasing revenue. As executive vice president, I was in charge of the whole shebang. Everyone answered to me. I made all the hard calls.

So why wasn't I called president? I decided to ask VF president and CEO Mackey McDonald.

"Hopefully, you guys think we are doing an excellent job out here," I said.

"Absolutely," he responded. "You are the best. We could not be more pleased."

"Wonderful," I said. "What I don't understand is that the guy I replaced had the title of president; he was screwing up the company and every indicator was pointed south, yet he had the title of president. Why not me?"

There was pride and practicality in my desire for what might seem to be lobbying for a mere title. Pride pushed me to be president. But the practical aspect weighed on me more. If I walked into a meeting with three colleagues who worked under me, and they were white, the people we were meeting assumed they had to be my bosses, that one of them must be the president.

"You got it, Larry," McDonald said. "Consider it done. We will put out a press release. Easy."

One more obstacle down.

9

NIKE TIME

*M*y first week at Nike, I was sitting in my office, and this tall guy walks by my door. Really tall. He leaned over and glanced in as he strolled by. I did a double take. Was that Patrick Ewing?

Later that same week I was walking across the Nike campus after work. The sun was setting on Beaverton, Nike's home seven miles west of downtown Portland. I must admit I had a hard time finding my way around Nike's campus, which back then was about seventy acres. The "campus" was Disneyland with sports stars instead of cartoon characters. I couldn't help but be a little amazed—the buildings looked like sculptures, the walkways wound through woods, the lake in the middle provided some sense of direction. I could have used a map, especially when the sun started to go down. I saw a couple of guys walking toward me. One of them had on a baseball cap turned to the back. They got a little closer. Was that the Seattle

Mariners center fielder? Yep, Ken Griffey Jr. He nodded. I nodded back.

Be cool.

Top athletes strolled around the Nike campus as if it were their personal playground, which it was. On any given afternoon you might see Serena Williams, John McEnroe, Michael Jordan, Dan Fouts, Bo Jackson, Mike Schmidt, or Charles Barkley showing up for a meeting or joining someone for lunch in the cafeteria. The staff was just cool about it. They barely even seemed to notice. In those early days, it was hard for me to be as cool. At Jantzen you might see a photo on the wall of Marilyn Monroe or Rita Hayworth wearing a bathing suit. That was about it. But I got used to it, and it quickly became normal.

When Don King showed up, even the most laid-back Nike folks lost their cool. I brought the legendary boxing promoter by for a meeting. He was interested in partnering with Nike, putting our trademark swoosh on boxing gloves, negotiating an endorsement for one of his fighters. He and I had gotten to know one another at Magic, the annual fashion trade show in Vegas.

"If you set me up with Phil Knight at Nike," he told me, "I'll do the rest."

I had arranged the meeting with Phil, so I walked him into the boss's office. Charlie Denson, then Nike brand president, walked by and did a double take.

Phil jumped up from behind his desk to greet King.

"Wait," the CEO said. "I'll be right back."

He went to get his assistant and said, "Can you take a picture of me and Don?"

We were talking trash and about set to talk business when she came back with a camera. "Stop the music," Phil said. She snapped a bunch of pictures. Knight stepped back and grinned. "The caption on the picture will be: 'The guy with the worst hair in sports. Pick one.'"

I HAD PICKED a good time to leave Jantzen. I had had a good run, but I was ready for bigger stakes.

When I took over as president, Jantzen was pulling a couple hundred million dollars a year, which was on the low end for a historic swimsuit maker. It had been one of the first sportswear companies to have stars endorse products, but it had gotten stale. It went from innovative to isolated, so to speak. My team and I really got things going with new products and a fresh approach to marketing with a total makeover, starting with fashion.

When I first hooked up with Brian Epstein on the women's swimwear side, we started brainstorming how to reposition our swimsuits.

"Let's get them into fashion shows," I suggested. "Nothing like a model in a swimsuit to get fashion writers' attention."

"Why not?" he said. "But how?"

"Let's figure out a way to show our new line at Fashion Week in New York," I said. "Swimwear is fashion."

Epstein didn't ask how I would pull it off. Frankly, I wasn't sure. But I was sure that this was where I wanted to be: strategizing and engineering the sell, breaking into a new market, building the brand. My deal with Epstein from the start was that I wanted to branch out from accounting to sales and marketing.

IT WAS NEVER just about finance for me, even back at Campbell's and Kraft. I always wanted to be on the marketing and business development side, where I could call the shots across the board. Product reviews. Sales calls. Marketing strategy. I was always looking beyond the numbers.

Jantzen still had a very powerful name, and I used it to get on the runway. We arranged and produced our own fashion show the first year, and Miss Universe walked down the aisle in one of our new suits. The second year Tyra Banks, on the brink of superstardom at twenty-three, strolled down the runway in strappy, black platform heels, sporting a Jantzen suit with yellow flowers against a black background that flowed into a skirt that landed just above her ankles. Her picture made the New York *Daily News*, and that suit made us a lot of money.

Parlaying the win in New York, we convinced VF to increase our budget to raise the profile of the brand. We delved into the product-development process. We brought in new, edgier fashion designers. We pushed them to shorten the window from design to manufacturing. We transformed the entire process from design to production to marketing.

When Jantzen's numbers started to improve and then headed

due north, the VF brass noticed. Our CEO, Larry Pugh, called after Fashion Week.

"I really like what you guys are doing," he said. "Keep it up."

BUT NO MATTER how well we did, we were always in the shadow of Nike, the other sports apparel company in Portland.

Jantzen was improving its game in women's swimwear, but Nike was in the major leagues, selling all types of sporting equipment, footwear, gear, and apparel worldwide, from its sprawling campus in Beaverton. Starting with its swoosh logo in the athletic shoe business in 1971, Nike had steadily grown into a marketing powerhouse. It had signed Michael Jordan to a sneaker deal in 1984, lucrative both for MJ and Nike. By 1990, Nike was the nation's largest athletic shoe and apparel manufacturer. In 1996, it brought on Tiger Woods to represent its golf line.

Never slowing down, Nike was determined to dominate the '96 Summer Olympics in Atlanta. That would require facing off with Reebok, the games' official sponsor.

At the same time, Epstein and I were also determined to keep developing new business opportunities, including making our mark at the Olympics. Jantzen had a fine market in suits you would wear on the beach or on a cruise or whatever, but we were ignoring the market share that focused on competition swimwear. It could be an obvious fit.

"Perfect opportunity for us to get into that area and increase our part of that market share," I told my team during one of our weekly strategy sessions. But how?

Then it dawned on me: Why not make a deal with Nike? We made swimsuits; Nike made athletic wear—but no swimwear. The fact that we were both right there in Portland would also make things easier. I figured we could do some sort of partnership or licensing deal with them. I took the idea straight to Jay Titsworth, who at that point was still my boss. I was pretty excited and paced around his office as I rolled out my idea. He sat back.

"Why would Nike want to do it?" he asked. "What's in it for them?" He gave a thumbs-down.

Undeterred, I investigated. Turned out Nike was looking for a company to partner with to make and market swimwear so they could have a bigger presence in the upcoming Olympics swimming competition. Nike's brand was big in the second week's track and field events. They wanted to make a splash in the first week's competition in the pool. They had been talking to companies like TYR that were already doing competition swimwear. Why not Jantzen?

I reached out to Mary Slayton, the Nike exec who was arranging the presentations, and asked if Jantzen could pitch. They were open to it, so we put together our presentation. It was my first time on the Nike campus. I had heard that it was a shrine to sports and athletics, but I was not prepared for the mecca we walked through that day. I kept my cool as I gave Jantzen its best shot. After I ran through the PowerPoint, I finished them off with an uppercut.

"You can connect with a company that's already in the competitive swimwear business," I said. I knew that TYR and Speedo had already presented. "But why would they be motivated to produce the best product for Nike? They would be cannibalizing their own products, eating into their own profits. Why would they want to do that? With Jantzen, you would be partnering with a company that knows how to make the best swimwear, but we do not have a competitive line. You fill a need for us; we fill a need for you. Perfect fit.

"Plus," I said, "we are right here in Portland. That makes everything easier and smoother."

After we left, Stephen Gomez, head of global apparel for Nike at the time, closed the door and took his seat at the head of the table. Days later someone on the Nike team told me Gomez said, "You know, you guys can keep looking, but it doesn't get any better than that."

We would end up doing the deal, and it's still in place today. It was one of the first licensing deals for both Nike and Jantzen. Both companies were determined to make it work. For us to do a licensing deal with Nike was huge.

By the time it actually got signed, I was running Jantzen as president. Stephen Gomez was still in charge of global apparel for Nike. I'll never forget showing up in Indianapolis for my first college swim meet. The Stanford swim team came out head to toe in Nike gear—the swoosh on caps and suits and slides. Our suits, their logo. And Nike dominated the '96 Olympics, the swoosh almost as universal as the Olympic rings. Gomez and I celebrated.

Gomez was a stand-up guy, very selfless, and totally devoted to giving back to the Portland community. We immediately found common ground. Gomez and I agreed that we would stay involved on a level where, if our respective teams couldn't work something out, then he and I would step in and make sure that it got done. We also agreed that about once every quarter or so we would get together and talk over what was going on with the business and discuss any issues that might come up.

We often had these meetings over dinner. The last time we had one, early in 1997, Gomez described some changes in Nike's business divisions. He went into great detail about how they were splitting off domestic U.S. apparel from the global division. And they needed someone to run this new operation. I left the restaurant and thought to myself: "I feel like I just got interviewed."

A couple of weeks later Gomez called me up to check in. Then he got to the point: "Would you ever consider coming over to work for Nike?"

I could have pondered the question and played hard to get.

"Definitely," I said.

After he hung up, I sat back and considered what was about to happen. Going from Jantzen to Nike to me was like going from playing in the D-League to the NBA. Jantzen was a relatively small company. It thought like a small company, and it operated like a small company. There was nothing small about Nike. They dominated athletic footwear, equipment, and sports apparel worldwide. Nike's swoosh was drilled into the global consciousness. I knew I could play in the big leagues. I was ready.

By that time, I was nearing the end of five years at Jantzen, the last three running the company. Jantzen was back. I had few regrets. But leaving a few people who had become important in my life was hard.

My first call was to CFO Jerry Johnson. I had been straight with him all along. He knew I had been talking to Nike. And he knew it would be a good move for me.

"Well, Miller, I'm not happy," he said, "but I can see why you would want to leap at that opportunity. There are endless possibilities over there in Beaverton."

STEPHEN GOMEZ HAD seen a few newcomers to Nike blow those opportunities. Before I started, he invited me for lunch in the Nike cafeteria.

"It's a pretty tight culture over here," he told me. "It can be hard on newcomers trying to break in. Give it time."

Gomez gave me a list of people who were essential to running Nike, the back-office stalwarts and operational folk who showed up and got things done, rather than the top suits.

"For your first month or so, just watch and listen," he said. "Learn as much as you can—before you try and change things."

Nike execs at the time were in the process of putting more emphasis on U.S. business. They had their global leadership team managing the U.S. as well, but it had grown to a point where they knew they needed a separate team to handle the domestic apparel business. I became the first head of the division, which was nearly a billion-dollar business at the time, with about six hundred employees.

Gomez remained head of global apparel, and as head of the U.S. division, I reported to him. I took his advice and visited every person on his list. It did take a month or two to settle in. I had inherited a strong team, and I added a few more members to firm it up even more. But I also inherited a culture and a system that needed change. Once I satisfied myself that I had listened and learned as much as I could under Gomez's guidance, I got to work.

PRODUCTION FIRST.

When I took the helm in 1997, the apparel "go-to-market" process took eighteen months, from design to production and marketing to delivery to stores. That was insane to me. We were essentially creating a product line that wouldn't hit the consumer for a year and a half. Who knew if market trends today might be the same in eighteen months? The marketplace moved too fast. We wouldn't be able to see results before planning the next season; we had no ability to respond to trends in the marketplace. Even at Jantzen we could get a new swimsuit from design to stores in six to nine months. Something was way off.

Nike had made its name in the performance footwear zone, and while we were producing and marketing athletic shoes, Nike led the market. Whatever it did set the tone.

But apparel was a different matter. It was much more dependent on style and fashion, which could change in a blink. When

I started to raise the distinction to my team and around the campus, I got a taste of what I was up against:

"Fashion," on the Nike campus, was the f-word.

NOT LONG AFTER I became head of apparel, I made a sales run to check out the Niketown store in San Francisco. I was walking down a women's footwear aisle when I saw this attractive young lady reach up and pull down a running shoe. She held it up and admired the shape and color. She was wearing black leggings and a purple racer-back top. She looked like a runner who cared about style—basically, our target consumer.

She took the shoe over to the apparel section. She walked from rack to rack, holding it up next to tops and hats and shorts. Her mouth turned down. I could see what she was thinking: "Nothing matches."

She turned back to the footwear aisle, replaced the shoe, and left the store.

I thought: "If she had found something she could wear with the shoes, we would have made a sale on both ends. She couldn't make a match, so we lost both sales."

I returned to Portland, described what I had witnessed, and told my team: "We have to figure out how to create apparel lines that make sense with our footwear." We were losing out on market share to urban apparel firms like FUBU and Cross Colours because they were making hip, cool, "urban" apparel and meeting that market. Why not Nike?

That placed me in the position of helping Nike develop a new strategy: we needed to maintain the performance market but also begin to embrace and serve the lifestyle market. Nothing happened fast at Nike, as Stephen Gomez had warned. I understood that. We started to bring together teams of designers and marketers from the performance side to collaborate with our apparel teams. Slowly, we worked on shortening production times, so we could "see" the market we would be selling into.

I WAS VERY aware that Nike had another, deeper problem: race. Which raised a question: Did they hire me because I'm Black?

In 1990, Reverend Jesse Jackson's PUSH civil rights organization had called for a boycott of Nike products. Rev. Jackson pointed out that Nike received 30 percent of its $6.8 billion athletic shoe revenue from Black dollars, yet it had no Black executives and invested little in the Black community. Phone calls to PUSH's Chicago headquarters were answered: "Operation PUSH—say no to Nike!"

Phil Knight reacted quickly with promises to hire minority executives and establish an outside, minority advisory board.

"We have increased the number of African-American executives in our ranks, and we need to keep increasing it," he said in a letter to Nike employees. "The same can be said of each minority group in this country—Hispanics, Asians, Native Americans. All should be represented at Nike, and we have a commitment to that."

Nike put no time line on its commitment.

When I arrived in 1997 as vice president and general manager of U.S. Apparel, I was Nike's first Black vice president, ever. There was noise on racial matters, but I wouldn't call it loud noise. Nike was selling to a Black athletic market, but that was not reflected by the internal organization. In short, our consumers were Black, but our executive leadership was predominantly white. Everyone was aware.

Nike had put John Thompson Jr., legendary coach of the Georgetown University basketball team, on its board of directors. John had earned that spot, both through his coaching and nurturing of superstar Black athletes like Patrick Ewing and Allen Iverson and through his advocacy for Black athletes in the NCAA. They also brought in Ron Williams as the head of diversity.

So, could being Black have had anything to do with my being hired as Nike's first VP of U.S. Apparel? You could make that case, but I had earned every promotion up the ladder and learned every business maneuver along the way. I had the academic letters behind my name, years toiling in the accounting side, and nearly a decade at the executive level doing deals, developing strategy, and executing it. Stephen Gomez and Nike didn't hire me because I was Black, but they didn't pass over me because of it, either—and that was the win.

Did the fact that I was Black, competent, and prepared for the opportunity contribute to Nike's success in dominating the sports apparel business? The company did have a need to understand the young consumer from the street, our principal market, as Black men and women from that demographic tend to be the trendsetters for the world. Black culture and particularly the inner-city streets set style trends, and the rest of the world usually follows. That was how athletic wear and sneakers became fashion, and baggy shorts went from the hood to the NBA and around the world. And I did happen to know something about that life. But that was my secret, one that kept getting tested.

ONE MORNING IN May 1999, about a year and a half into my time at Nike, a formal invitation arrived on my desk. It was addressed by hand, in calligraphy, on that cream-colored, heavy paper envelope that screams money. It almost looked like a wedding invitation. I turned it over. Embossed on the back flap were three words: "The White House."

"What could this be?" I wondered.

I always showed up at the Nike campus first thing in the morning, often before eight. I liked the silence and private moments before the day got crazy. I could breathe better in the calm. Not a soul was around. I sat back and opened the envelope.

The notecard invited me to a private dinner in New York to raise funds for President Bill Clinton's library. He was close to completing his term and already hard at work making sure his presidential library would be well endowed. It was signed: "Bill and Hillary."

First, I tried to figure out who had wired up the invitation and why, since I was not exactly a deep-pocketed sports magnate. Then, I tried to figure out whether I should accept and risk getting busted by the Secret Service background check. For the nearly two decades since the birth of the secret that day in

1982 (when the Arthur Andersen partner withdrew his job offer because I had chosen to reveal my felonious past), I had existed in a realm of risk and reward, measuring the risk of having the secret revealed against the reward of moving up in the business world.

Not a day went by when I didn't feel split in two: half the successful executive, half the gangster that none of my fellow executives knew. I lived with being two people, looking at the world from two sets of eyes, wondering what this corporate world would think of me if they knew my secret.

This invitation raised the stakes to the highest yet: risk being found out by a Secret Service background check versus the reward of meeting the president and first lady at an intimate dinner. My stomach immediately knotted up.

My assistant showed up around nine. I tried to regain my cool. I handed the invite to her.

"Can you see what they will need for a security check?" I asked.

WHILE SHE CHECKED, I worried. The secret's malignant grip on my life had grown more toxic. Dark dreams fueled paranoia during the day, which made the next night's dreams even darker.

I still wonder why no employer ever asked me about my early life, or how it never came up over the course of my career that I had been convicted and served time.

As I moved further up in the corporate world and into the executive realm, the security checks seemed to matter less. I don't even recall filling out paperwork when I made the move from Kraft Foods in Philly to Jantzen in Portland. I accepted the controller job on a handshake.

In the digital sphere, where every Google search could turn up unsavory facts from anyone's past, how could my history in the criminal justice system not have surfaced? I had just about lived behind bars since the early arrests that put me into Philly's criminal justice system before I turned thirteen. There was the guilty plea for second-degree murder in 1966 and the incarceration at Camp Hill, via Eastern State Penitentiary and Holmesburg Prison. And the felonies for armed robbery in 1975 that landed me in Graterford for nearly five years.

How did the lid stay on those records? I entertained two possibilities:

The early arrests and the following felonies came at a time when arrest records were written on 3×5 cards or typed out on a typewriter and carbon copied, then filed away in metal cabinets or on shelves buried in archives. Maybe they were never digitized. If they were digitized, they were never entered into public databases. Or they were misfiled. Or they were lost.

Or, I could chalk it up to a blessing. I was not about to waste my time asking why.

THAT MORNING IN 1999, I found myself confronting the secret in very real terms. I had succeeded in running Nike's U.S. Apparel division. Greater opportunities lay ahead. I was on a roll, so to speak. Should I accept the invitation to the Clinton dinner? Or play it safe and stay in my lane? It would be a small gathering of about forty people. I was scared to death at the prospect of my secret being discovered.

I put off responding.

"Hey," my assistant said one morning, "the organizers of the Clinton dinner keep calling. They want to know whether you are going to attend."

"What's the story on security? What do they need?" I asked.

"Social security number and date of birth," she said.

Secret Service also required my last two addresses. I could give them two in Portland: an apartment and our house. No need to take anyone back to Philly. I thought about it for a week.

"All right," I told my assistant. "Accept the invitation and deal with Secret Service."

My attitude at this point was it was worth the risk. If something happened, and law enforcement types started to dig into my past, I could deal with it. No matter what I had acquired, or how people viewed me in the corporate world, these things don't make me who I am. They didn't define me. If it all went away, I would be okay.

Wouldn't I?

TWO WEEKS LATER I got the "all clear." The White House called with details about the dinner, and I flew to New York with a mix of anticipation and anxiety.

That night in New York turned out to be one of the most amazing nights of my life. Only in Manhattan. The night had started around six o'clock with a fund-raising reception Derek Jeter was hosting for his foundation. It was close to Times

Square. Plenty of Yankees showed up. I spent time with Jeter, Joe Torre, and Darryl Strawberry. The Yankees would go on to win the World Series that season, again.

Around 8:30 I walked from Jeter's event up to the Clinton dinner, which was held at a small French restaurant in Midtown called La Grenouille. The closer I got, the more anxious I became. I would have to go through security at the door. What if they stopped me? Every step I wondered: "Why am I putting myself through this?"

Sure enough, stone-faced guys with earpieces wired to communication devices tucked into their suits stood at the entrance. I handed over my driver's license to a woman who was probably a publicist. She glanced at the picture and up at me. She smiled. "Welcome, Mr. Miller. Here's your wristband." To say I was relieved does not even come close.

Fifteen minutes later Bill and Hillary arrived. They had rearranged the dining room with four round tables that each sat ten people. I found my name card, took a seat, and looked to my right: Hillary Rodham Clinton. She gave me that big, warm smile and met my stare with her piercing but inviting blue eyes. I was pleased to sit by the president's wife, but I was not in the kind of awe that would make me stumble over my words or anything. I had just left a party with Derek Jeter and his crowd of stars. That is the world I live in. If anything, I was still a little nervous about security.

The first lady and I talked all night about sports and running clothes and Nike stars like MJ. The Monica Lewinsky scandal was off the front pages but still on everyone's mind. The last thing she wanted to talk about was politics or anything about the White House. I must have been the perfect dinner partner. Turns out Russell Simmons and I were the only Black people in the room. I even had a chance to talk with the president. He was friendly and smooth. I witnessed just how smooth.

After the dinner, the president took a few questions.

A young woman stood up, brushed back her hair, and looked up at Bill Clinton. She looked like she was in her midtwenties. "Mr. President, I'm really interested in politics," she said. "Do you have any suggestions for me?"

"Well," he said, "you should definitely consider connecting with the right people. Look into interning. You could intern for me."

"He didn't just say that," I thought. I just about spit out my chocolate mousse! "This dude is a cold-blooded Mack!" I thought. And he just kept it moving, like, "Next question." He didn't even bat an eye.

Bill is wild.

Once I made it through that level of scrutiny, I guessed I was okay. The president was at one table in this tiny restaurant and Hillary was at another, and somehow, I ended up seated right next to her. For me to clear that kind of a security check, I shouldn't worry that much.

They were still there when I left around 11:30. I walked to another venue where Spike Lee was having a premiere party for his movie *Summer of Sam*. Me and Spike had gotten to know one another over the years. We're still good friends.

Weary from a wonderful New York night, I settled into bed back at my hotel and fell into a deep sleep. I woke up in the middle of the night—back in jail. No relief.

10

BRANDING JORDAN

*O*ne day early in the summer of 1998 Phil Knight called me into his office. His Ray-Ban shades hid his eyes. He seemed relaxed, but he was squeezing the hell out of one of those soft stress balls.

"Jordan's planning to retire from the NBA," he said. "We know this. What we don't know is whether we retire Air Jordan when he's done playing."

Phil was about sixty at the time, but he neither looked nor acted it. The man who started Nike by selling running shoes out of the trunk of his Plymouth Valiant in 1964 still had the heart and drive of an entrepreneur. Among other things, we shared two essential ingredients for success in business: mutual trust and respect.

"I would hate to just say bye to MJ and Air Jordan," he said.

He was doing all the talking. I just listened, but I was hardly shocked by what he was saying. Nike execs had been contemplating life after Jordan's retirement and planning how to keep his shoe sales strong. I also knew I was in the running to build a new brand around Jordan.

Air Jordan sneakers didn't make Nike Nike. But Air Jordan basketball sneakers were more than a cultural, style, and marketing phenomenon. The Air Jordan franchise had become a serious source of revenue since Nike introduced the shoes in 1984. Across the globe, MJ was the most popular athlete. From the rough parts of Chicago and L.A. to the gaming tables of Macau and teeming streets of Hong Kong, people lined up to buy the next Jordans and cleared shelves within minutes. We had just rolled out Air Jordan 14, a racing design influenced by a Ferrari that reflected Jordan's love for fast cars and motorsports. Stores sold out of them in days.

"Will we make a 15?" Phil asked.

"Of course," I said. "No doubt."

"Good," he said. "You make it happen."

With that, Phil Knight blessed splitting off Jordan Brand as its own division, with me as president.

"How are you going to pull this off?" he asked.

Good question. Barely two years into my career at Nike, I had been asked for the second time to create and run a brand-new division. You could say I was ready for another opportunity. You could also say I was nervous.

THE FIRST TIME Michael Jordan and I met was in a Seattle hotel suite in the spring of 1998, a few months before my session with Phil Knight.

Designers and marketers were giving MJ a chance to preview the next Air Jordan shoe, set for release that October. The
preview turned into a redesign session. Nike execs and designers had let Jordan know that I wanted to sit in. I hoped to discuss apparel and how the brand could begin to cash in on some
of the market share we were losing out on to urban apparel
brands like FUBU and Cross Colours. The meeting had already
started when I walked in. Jordan was sitting on a couch, looking around at the gathering of executives and designers. He
looked up and smiled at the new guy.

"Hey, LM," he said after I was introduced. "What's up?
What's happening today?"

I smiled, held up my hand, and said, "Hey, MJ." I slid into a
seat, took it all in, but didn't say a word.

Before the birth of Jordan Brand, I hadn't spent much time
with Michael Jordan. Though we knew of each other, we had
never met one-on-one or sat down to talk. His shoe was part
of Nike, so I played a role in marketing it in North America—
along with fifty other products. But that didn't mean I got to
hang out with the guy whose name was on the sneaker. Jordan
was playing eighty-two games in the NBA regular season, plus
off-season workouts, preseason games, and the playoffs. He and
the Chicago Bulls were coming off two straight NBA championship seasons (and six overall) and were about to begin their final
championship run, the "Last Dance." Not to mention he had a
family. And there was golf.

"Let's take a look at the shoe," Jordan said. He was in town
to play against Seattle that night. He stood up to his full six feet

six inches. He looked chill and relaxed in warm-ups. At thirty-six, MJ was still in his prime—and carried himself that way. He had been ranked the world's highest paid athlete, counting his salary and income from endorsements. "I'm not so sure about a few things," he added.

He picked up the sneaker, raised it up to eye level, and examined it, as if he were critiquing a small piece of art, which his shoe was for millions of sneaker heads. He squinted. His mouth turned down. Things were going south, fast. Marketing guys were singing the sneaker's praises. MJ frowned.

I was in the back thinking: "I'm the new guy on the block. I'm just going to keep quiet. But to me, that shoe would look better if the tongue was black."

Meanwhile, MJ was holding the shoe up and turning it around in his hands. "Look man," he finally said. "Can we make the tongue black on this? Let's keep everything else the same."

No problem, of course. MJ called the shots, and everybody smiled.

After they were all done and the room emptied out, we sat down—MJ and I—for the first time.

"I could see you weren't into the white tongue either," he said. We laughed, then we discussed brand apparel and how we could better connect it to the urban market.

I shared my thoughts around Nike product lines and the potential of the Jordan Brand. He listened. I rolled out my views on how Nike needed to start considering style, fashion even, in developing new apparel lines—and how they needed to be aligned with the performance market, especially shoes. He looked at me closely, his eyes hooded, skeptical.

"Man," he finally said, "we've been trying to do this shit for the last fourteen years. What makes you think this is going to be different?"

I explained how our competitors were looking to our footwear catalogs, eyeballing our colorways, and designing their apparel to match. "We're missing out," I said. "They're stealing our best ideas and using them to beat us." That got his attention. "We can fix that."

Was I a little anxious? Maybe. Did I show it? Hell no. Motto on the streets of West Philly and in prison: come off as weak and you're done. Not only was I immune to Jordan's teasing, but I knew I could sell his shoes to a broader market. I believed in Jordan and his product. If I could get behind it, I could sell it. If I was in, I was in all the way. I never did anything half-assed, from the days I was hustling as a kid to selling swimsuits for Jantzen.

"Look, if you can pull this off, I'm with you," he said. Then he went off on beating the competition. It was my first indication that the competitive instincts that drove Jordan to NBA championships would translate well to the business world. MJ wanted to win customers, design great product, dominate the competition.

"That's all I needed to hear you say."

"I got you," he said. "We're good."

I had Michael Jordan. Then I had Phil Knight. I was very good. Starting with the black tongue on the white shoe.

REGARDLESS OF THE color or trim, once Jordan stopped floating to the rim and dunking the ball, would anyone want to buy his sneakers? The industry wondered if the new Jordan Brand would survive when he was no longer dropping back to sink a buzzer-beating three-pointer. How would we keep the brand alive after MJ quit running them up and down the court?

Underlying those doubts, could a Black executive manage and develop what could become a new global brand?

In many ways Jordan Brand was the first of its kind, a sneaker not just bearing the name of an athlete, but a shoe worn by the athlete himself, who happened to be an outrageously successful athlete, perhaps the best ever. Keep in mind that when Nike debuted the inaugural Air Jordans in 1984, they violated the league's uniform rules. Players were required to wear shoes that matched their uniforms and the shoes their teammates wore. The shoes were black and red, out of step with the NBA's standard white sneakers. The league fined Jordan $5,000 every time he wore them on the court. Nike played the rule violation as the perfect marketing tool. Jordan kept wearing the "illegal" shoe, and the first Air Jordans became known as "The Banned." And they took flight from there.

As for me and the iconic shoe, there were thirteen Air Jordans before I even showed up at Nike. I was a latecomer to the brand.

Up until Jordan's retirement in 1999, the formula had been: we design this really cool-looking shoe and promote it with some eye-catching marketing with Spike Lee or Bugs Bunny or somebody, and, of course, Michael is wearing his shoe on the court. Talk about free advertising. Fans will never forget MJ making that winning shot in the 1998 finals against the Utah Jazz, dropping a twenty-foot jumper and falling to the floor, red Jordan 14s up in the air, forever known as the "Last Shot."

Now we had to remove that last part of the formula.

A lot of people in the sports apparel game said, "Well, they had a nice run but it's over." Our competitors counted us out.

PHIL KNIGHT CALLING me into his office mid-1998 and telling me I would become president of Jordan Brand had a backstory that began long before I met MJ that day in Seattle.

It was the culmination of a months-long process to reorganize Nike's business divisions, once again. Nike leadership had called in Andy Mooney to direct the reorganization. He had been with Nike for decades and risen to chief marketing officer in the United States, then went on to work for Disney and then became CEO of Fender, but he had started out in accounting way back. Andy and I bonded over the fact that we both had started with back-office numbers and navigated our way into the executive ranks.

Mooney came up with a plan to divide a portion of the Nike enterprise into three Category Business Units: All Conditions Gear, which included all-weather sportswear and shoes; Golf, because it had specific performance gear and style, with global reach; and Jordan Brand, including all things MJ, from shoes to apparel and anything else we could brand with the "Jumpman" logo. Each would be an operating unit unto itself. This categorical approach would eventually spread to the rest of the Nike enterprise.

Once Mooney pitched his plan and Nike accepted it, the question was who was going to run Jordan.

He spoke to Howard White for some guidance. "H," as everyone called him, had been close to MJ since Michael first signed with Nike in 1984.

"I know just the guy," H responded.

Howard White had been a star player at the University of Maryland in the seventies. He is an enduring, trusted figure at Nike and beyond to the greater sporting world. Starting with MJ, H had carved out a unique and essential place for himself at Nike. He basically invented Nike's Athletic Relations Department, the unit that treated sports stars—largely African American— as human beings rather than commodities. Moses Malone, Charles Barkley, Deion Sanders—they all love H. Nike could be strictly business; Howard was a friend, a mentor, the guy who helped young athletes adjust to newfound wealth. H also became my partner and close confidant. Without H, I would not have been able to do what I did with building the Jordan Brand.

H's relationship with MJ was his first, longest lasting, and most substantial in the business. But that was not why H and I got along. He and I met during the '96 Olympics in Atlanta, when Jantzen sponsored a swim team. When I arrived at Nike I used to swing by his office, both to visit H and because it was usually jumping. I was likely to run into some NBA superstar.

Apparently, H had a good feeling about me.

"So," Andy Mooney asked, "who's the guy to run Jordan Brand?"

"Gotta be Larry Miller," H responded. "He's the one."

Without my even knowing it, H had made the case for making me president of Jordan Brand to MJ, Phil Knight, and the other Nike execs. He had to get to MJ at the height of his final "Last Dance" season with the Bulls. Once everyone was on board, Mooney took me to dinner to ask if I would be willing to take on Jordan Brand.

Again, I stayed cool, but what an opportunity!

I told Mooney about a dream I had had about working with Michael Jordan even before I got to Nike.

"One night, a year before I started at Nike, when I was still running Jantzen, Michael Jordan showed up in a dream," I said. "He and I were meeting around a table, he in his Bulls uniform and I in my tailored suit. He flashed that Jordan smile, and he gave me one warning: 'Glad you made the meeting, Larry. Never be late. Never.'"

"It's meant to be," Mooney said.

What I didn't tell Mooney about was the dream that took me down the next night.

The nightmare took off where the earlier dream ended: Jordan was warning me not to be late for a meeting. I was on my way to meet him when a bunch of men grabbed me, threw me into a car, and took me to court.

"You don't understand, Judge," I said. "I have to be at a meeting." Then I was in a holding cell. I was wearing a suit. My hands were cuffed behind my back. Everyone was staring at me. "This is a big mistake," I said. "Please let me out. You don't understand. Michael Jordan is waiting for me. I can't be late!" No one responded. I kept yelling. All I got was blank stares. Then I woke up, gasping for air, wondering whether I was still in a dream.

When I settled down, a more pressing question came to mind: Could I pull off Jordan Brand? I had presided over Jantzen and begun to work my way up in Nike. But this would be different—essentially creating a startup within a huge company set in its ways and somewhat skeptical.

RIGHT OUT OF the gate, I knew we had to launch Jordan Brand with a major event and a strong, distinctive advertising campaign. The first fourteen Air Jordans sold themselves while Michael Jordan was on the court. How would we continue to grow the brand when he retired from professional basketball? Would 15 have the same prestige?

"We're going to build a new brand," I would tell my colleagues at Nike, "bigger and better than before."

They would smile and say, "Good luck." As in: fat chance.

That doubt about Jordan's own brand seemed to have seeped into Nike's advertising agency, Wieden+Kennedy. Based in Portland, it had grown up with Nike. When we approached them to build a new campaign, their reaction did not seem very energetic. We got: "Oh, yeah—we'll try to figure something out on Jordan." We were flying back to Portland from Houston in Phil Knight's plane—just me, H, and Phil. H believed in the possibilities of the brand. I sat next to Phil in the back of the plane and told him my concerns. I felt that we needed a new approach to marketing.

"All right," Phil said, "but before you make any change, let me know." So, we went out and interviewed a bunch of other agencies.

Phil called me one day. "Wieden+Kennedy is opening up a New York office. I want you to at least go and talk with those guys before you make a move."

We met, and I immediately felt the energy their new team brought to launching and supporting Jordan Brand. We agreed to work together and built the launch around the "Overjoyed" commercial featuring star athletes of the day giving way to Michael Jordan, dressed in casual clothes, leaving the viewer with a sense that MJ was still the force behind the sports scene, even as he was yielding his role to other champions.

We took off after that. People still talk about the launch event. We nailed it.

That night, though, was capped off by another crushing nightmare.

IT WOULD HAVE been a mistake to try and get Michael Jordan's attention to help launch Jordan Brand while he was in the midst of competing for the Bulls' sixth NBA title in the spring of 1998. When he did show up on campus after the Bulls prevailed over the Utah Jazz, Michael said to me: "You know, I could not sleep at all the whole two weeks of the finals."

But a few weeks after the Bulls won and celebrated, MJ started showing up on the campus to work on vision and strategy. The vision was clear: to create a premium brand of athletic footwear and apparel, within sports culture, beginning with basketball but branching out to other sports. At every stage we would define anything with the Jumpman as exceptional, superior. We identified and connected to our core consumers, the inner-city youth, but we also looked beyond. Why not baseball? Boxing?

It was up to me to execute the vision with a solid strategy.

One of the things I brought to the table was a different perspective. I was pushing for us to move faster, but we needed to work on the logistics first.

I decided to put Gentry Humphrey, the best footwear production person in the business, in charge of footwear *and* apparel. A month later he showed up in my office. "Now I understand," he said. "I've been basically killing the apparel guys with my production schedule."

Hell, when I started at Jordan Brand, we didn't even have anyone in charge of operations. I said to my team: "You can have the best design and market it well, but if you can't get it to consumers, how do you make a sale?"

I needed Chuck Smith. He had been at Jantzen before he moved on to Nike. Like Gentry, he was the top man in the game. Our system started to work more smoothly, product development took less time, footwear and apparel started to show up in sync. Higher revenues followed.

Despite our success and the backing of Phil Knight, two years into the startup that was Jordan Brand I began to have my doubts about our potential for success within Nike. We saw Nike as the battleship and us at Jordan Brand as a PT boat.

I had become frustrated with the pace.

ONE WEEKEND IN 2002, my dear friend Raj Shah invited me to dinner. He and his brother, Akhil, had arrived in Seattle in the 1990s and started up fashion and clothing lines. Their Shah Safari brand was becoming a huge success worldwide. Raj and I had become very close friends over the years, and he asked me to come over and run their sports apparel side as they expanded globally.

They made an interesting and generous offer. And I was vulnerable. Even though it would have required a move to Seattle, I considered Raj's offer for a few weeks. I called him up.

"I'm in," I said. We started looking for a place in Seattle.

The next day I called Phil Knight's assistant and told her I had a personal matter to discuss. She got me right into the chairman's office.

"Personal matter, huh?" he said as soon as I walked inside. "Not sure I like the sound of that."

"I got offered a job outside of Nike," I said. I didn't feel it necessary to offer up any details.

"Really?" he said. Nike's top executives rarely left, and if they did, they rarely returned. There wasn't much discussion. "Is it money?"

"No," I said. "It's Nike's way of dealing—or not dealing—with Jordan Brand. There are people who are blocking us."

Phil ran a relaxed shop and that was reflected in his office and how he dealt with us. He came to the office in sweatshirts, jeans, and sneakers. I'm not sure the dude owns a tie. Once I walked by and he was on all fours on the floor, pushing a peanut across the rug with his nose. He'd lost a bet to an admin on a

University of Oregon vs. Oregon State football game, and he was paying up. But when I came to him to tell him Nike was getting in the way of Jordan Brand, he straightened up behind his desk and started asking questions.

"Look, Phil," I said at one point, "I feel like you asked me to do something—to build MJ and his brand into a substantial division of Nike. I also feel that people keep putting up roadblocks that get in the way of our achieving that. It's beyond frustrating."

Phil figured I was already out the door.

"Okay," he said, "if that's what you feel like you have to do, I understand. It would be a sad day for me, personally, and it would be a sad day for Nike.

"And if it doesn't work out, you can always come back."

That, in itself, was a gift. People were rarely invited back. I returned to my office feeling good that I would be leaving on good terms.

The phone rang.

"Larry Miller."

"It's Phil."

I responded, "What's up?"

"It would be a mistake for Nike—and for you—if you leave. Give me an opportunity to try and keep you with us. Let me work on it over the weekend, and let's meet on Monday."

Truth is, I didn't want to leave. I was frustrated as hell, but I also knew we had started something that I hadn't been able to finish. We had made progress. We were on the cusp of getting Jordan Brand in position for steady growth—even exponential growth. And Phil Knight was integral to that.

I felt close to Phil. He was the rare breed of corporate leader who was accessible and trusting. If I needed to talk to Phil, I would show up at the Nike cafeteria and look for him in his booth, reading the newspaper and eating a sandwich. I could slip into a seat, and we would get into it. His way of leading was to choose the right people for the right jobs and give them the resources and space to be successful. Replace them if they didn't measure up, of course, but trust them until that moment. I always thought Phil Knight had my back, and that gave me confidence to execute at the top level.

"You got it, Phil," I said. "Talk on Monday."

I can't say the weekend was pleasant. I had already told the family we were moving to Seattle, and Carol was up for the change. We had already picked out our new home. But when Phil Knight asked for time, the least I could do was give him a couple of days.

First thing Monday, Phil got on the phone and asked me to come over again. We got down to specifics about what I believed stood in the way of Jordan Brand's success. They were granular but crucial matters of design, logistics, and marketing dollars. I gave him example after example.

"We can address them all," he said. "Trust me."

Phil might show his laid-back demeanor to the world, but he can be persuasive when he wants something, or somebody, and he clearly wanted me to stay.

"And I know you said this isn't about money, but I can sweeten the pot, as well."

Phil's word was good enough for me. I knew I faced a lot of backtracking with Raj and my family, but I decided to stay with

Nike. One person I didn't have to tell was Michael Jordan. I had decided to discuss it first with Phil.

MJ never knew I had had one foot out the door.

MICHAEL JORDAN'S BUSINESS expertise is not well known. He gets a bad, undeserved rap on his little-known philanthropic side as well.

People expected MJ to give back to the community; he didn't need any pressure to meet his own expectations. As soon as MJ officially retired in January 1999, he directed us to focus funds on education—beginning with Jordan Fundamentals, which put $1 million a year into the hands of classroom teachers for books or supplies. That grew into Jordan Brand Wings scholarships that pay full rides for an average of thirty students a year, and growing. The brand's capacity for giving back has continued to grow from there. We never made a big deal about how much we gave and to whom. MJ was the same way with his personal philanthropy. Neither he nor the brand believed we had to pound our chests and seek approval. It's safe to say MJ always gave millions of dollars in personal funds every year.

Personally, shortly after I moved to Portland, I aligned myself with Self Enhancement, Inc. (SEI), a program founded in 1981 that provided academic support and a variety of services for Portland's African-American families in need. I showed up, served on the board, contributed funds, and made sure its founder, Tony Hopson, was well connected with Nike, including the time I sat him next to Phil when Roy Jones Jr. came to Portland for a fight.

"You sure I got the right seat?" Tony asked me.

He came away from the fight with a new supporter and a hefty contribution.

ROY JONES DIDN'T just show up in Portland in September 2002 to defend his light-heavyweight title by accident.

I have been a boxing fan my whole life. Coming up in Philly does that to you. It is my favorite sport. We knew we had to expand Jordan Brand beyond basketball shoes and apparel. We knew we needed to broaden the athletes on the Jordan Brand team. Shortly after taking over Jordan Brand, I was watching Roy Jones box his way to another belt on cable when it hit me: boxing!

My first call was to Roy Jones Jr. "We want to bring you on as a Jordan Brand member, the first in boxing. Are you interested?"

Roy was in. Then we brought on Andre Ward, an athlete who represented all that we had hoped to project: he was a champion, on the rise in the middleweight division, pursuing excellence in and out of the ring. He would go on to an undefeated record of 32-0 and become one of my good friends.

In addition to being pound for pound the best boxer in the world, Roy Jones met all of those marks as well. He called me up in the summer of 2002.

"Hey, I've got a fight coming up," he said, "and I would love to do it in Portland."

It was scheduled to be a defense of his world light-heavyweight title against Clinton Woods. A London venue had fallen through. Roy, an exception among boxers, promoted his own fights.

"I'll put up most of the money," he said, "if Nike can kick in some funds. You'll get it back."

I took the deal to Nike brand president Charlie Denson.

"Good for the brand—good for the city," I said.

Nike was in for $200,000 up front with a guaranteed return. Since Roy was a Jordan Brand athlete, we set up a training facility on the Nike campus, and we invited people to come in and see "Pound for Pound" work out and prepare for a fight. Weeks before the match, the Rose Garden was sold out. But there was more.

"Y'know," Roy told me, "I'm tired of all of these advertisements for beer all over the ring and on the mat. Why not put Jumpman center ring?"

Say no more. When the bell rang, and Roy tapped gloves with Clinton Woods to start the fight, they started circling around our logo in a boxing ring for the first time. It would not be the last. Phil Knight sat ringside. It might have been the highest-grossing event ever for the Rose Garden at the time. My phone lit up after. People loved it.

Roy took Woods out in the sixth round when his corner threw in the towel. It was the first time Nike got into the boxing promotion game, but it wasn't the last time the Jumpman got into the ring.

EVERY TIME I headed back east for a meeting in New York or D.C., I did my best to stop in at Graterford to see Brother Wazir. He was going through a long stretch of bad luck in his effort to gain release from his life sentence. It brought me peace to spend time with him. It reconnected me to such an important and formative part of my life. It also gave me a break from living two lives. And reminded me that I had committed myself to seeing that Brother Wazir became a free man.

II

JAIL BLAZERS

Coming up in Philly, I knew Portland, Oregon, for two things: Nike and the Trail Blazers, a troubled NBA team.

From 1983 to 2003, the Trail Blazers made it to the playoffs twenty-one times, but they won only two conference championships in that time. Clyde "the Glide" Drexler had been one of my favorite all-stars; he took the Blazers to the NBA finals against MJ and the Bulls in 1992. And lost. By the time I got to Portland, Clyde was long gone, and the franchise was in the can, but I still loved going to the Rose Garden arena to catch a game. I would request Nike's courtside seats when Kobe or Shaq came to town. When the Bulls played the Blazers, I would get a chance to see MJ wear Air Jordans on the court.

It was a win-win.

But the Trail Blazers weren't winners in those days, especially off the court. Some of the players were troublemakers and known for having trouble with the law. Players had been arrested for everything from drug possession to attempted rape and domestic violence. The team had even fined a player $250,000 for such behavior.

The Trail Blazers became known around the league as the Jail Blazers. Embarrassed by their hometown team, many Portland fans quit coming to their games. Sitting courtside and looking up at an empty arena, I would occasionally see owner Paul Allen, the billionaire who made his fortune by cofounding Microsoft with his childhood buddy Bill Gates. Paul would look up at the empty seats and shake his head.

ONE EVENING IN March 2007, I was having dinner with my buddy Tony Hopson of SEI at the arena before a game. We were in the Rose Room, a private dining room for sponsors and season ticket holders.

"Are we gonna win tonight?" Tony asked as he cut into a steak. "Or just get in trouble?"

Sarah Mensah took a seat beside me. She had been working in the Trail Blazers front office since 1993, on her way to becoming chief operating officer. She seemed unsettled.

"We're facing some changes," she said. "The Trail Blazers are not renewing Steve Patterson's contract." Patterson had been presiding over the team since 2003, when the Blazers started to fall apart. When he left, the team had a record of 24-34.

"We are looking for his replacement," Sarah said. "Got any ideas?"

I barely shrugged. Tony nudged me.

"Man," Tony said, "you should throw your hat in the ring."

I tossed that off as a cool thing one friend says to another. What did I know about selling tickets to pro basketball games? The business side of running an NBA franchise seemed, literally, out of my league.

Plus, I was riding high at the time. Jordan Brand had taken off and was growing every quarter. Why would I want to be president of a failing NBA franchise?

"Nope," I said. "Not interested. I don't know Paul Allen. And I'm good at Nike."

THINGS WERE BETTER than good at Jordan Brand for the first seven years.

Air Jordan 15 was the first shoe Michael Jordan would not be wearing on the court. It was also the first sneaker designed, marketed, and sold under the new corporate division I was overseeing—so we had to roll it out without a hitch. Legendary shoe designer Tinker Hatfield had put together one of his best designs, in my opinion. He was inspired in part by NASA's rocket-powered X-15 fighter jet. For the first official Jordan Brand release, it was perfect. It flew off the shelves.

Once MJ had retired in early 1999, he had started to meet with us on the campus. Born and raised in North Carolina, Michael had made his family's new home in Chicago.

"Come on out to our place," he said. "You can stay with us in the guest house."

Portland to Chicago became a routine run in those early days.

The visits were regular opportunities for MJ and me and some members of the team to talk over vision and strategy. Michael was involved with raising his children and was still an elite athlete, committed to staying in top shape, but he also immersed himself in the business end. We spent hours—days—sitting around his kitchen table with MJ at the head, spreading out profit and loss statements, discussing new product lines, tossing around fresh designs and ideas for wider markets. MJ understood more about Jordan Brand than some people realized. And he is just as competitive a businessman as he was a player. He always pushed us to be better, do more.

Before I came on board, Michael had helped choose the five young players who became the first Team Jordan for his self-named brand: first Ray Allen, then Derek Anderson, Eddie Jones, Vin Baker, and Michael Finley. We were solidifying the partnership and camaraderie that had started that day around the conference table at the Seattle hotel talking about the tongue color of the 14s. And now we were seeing Jumpman colors on more than shoes.

Once Phil Knight had pulled me back from leaving Nike, he also followed through and cleared away any roadblocks to our growth. That allowed us to more aggressively play out my hunch that Michael Jordan's connection to our basic market in the inner cities could expand from footwear to apparel. Footwear always dominated our production and marketing, but every year we added more product to go along with the shoes.

Back in Beaverton, I was hard at work building the organization behind the brand. From the minute I stepped on campus every morning, I was making decisions, or at least influencing decisions. To succeed, I had to use all of the experience and skills that I had picked up from Campbell Soup, Jantzen, and my first years at Nike. And my years behind bars at Graterford State Penitentiary.

With so much coming at me, I distilled my management philosophy down to two essential practices.

First, I put the right people in the right jobs. Choosing the right person required more than reading a résumé. In that role I needed to see through the B.S., ascertain whether the person would give their all to the team, and look for honesty and forthrightness.

Once I put the right person in the job, I gave them support, direction, and strategy, then got out of the way so they could do their jobs. I did not micromanage, and that has worked for the most part. Here is how I look at it: Everybody on the team has an important part to play. I'm just another player on the team. For us to win, everybody has to do their part and feel comfortable about doing their part. But I am the boss. If my philosophy doesn't work for the people I put in place, then they need to move on and try somewhere else. I will help them out with that part, too.

From the top, I set a tone of hard-core, unwavering belief in what we were selling, in this case the brand—from toe to head. I could always sell anything I truly believed in. I was 100 percent committed to selling fish for the Nation. That extended to selling myself. From one promotion to the next, I had to believe the things I was saying and believe that I could actually do the things I was saying I could do. And I worked hard to make that true.

That's what has helped me be successful. I connect with the right people and make them believe we are working toward the same goal. And if you work with me, I've got your back. We're in this together. I communicate that to the people on any team I put together. Believe what we are selling.

That's always how I looked at it. It set a baseline of respect and trust.

Our vision, strategy, and dedication began to produce results—shocking increases, actually. We started doubling Jordan Brand revenue year to year at first, on average. That brought our revenues for Nike close to $1 billion in 2007.

Those first eight years guiding Jordan Brand were a success for Nike, but they were also good for me and my family. I traveled plenty, but I tried to be around for important events in my kids' lives. Laila had come out a few times to visit.

Life was good. Nike was my home. I always felt it was a place where I could be myself, as long as I was making a contribution.

I was not looking for change.

WE WERE GETTING up from the table and heading to the court when Tony Hopson got back on me about running the NBA franchise.

"Don't be crazy," he said. "Why not look into it?"

Sarah, who I had known for a few years, agreed.

"Look," she said, "Tod Leiweke has come down from Seattle

to run the team until we find a new president." Leiweke was CEO of Vulcan Sports and Entertainment, a portion of the investment company Paul Allen founded with his sister Jody, to oversee his ventures. That put Leiweke in charge of all of Allen's arenas, the Trail Blazers, the NFL Seattle Seahawks, and the MLS Seattle Sounders. "Tod has no interest or time in managing the Blazers, so he's pretty eager to replace Patterson. You would be ideal."

"I'm not interested," I said.

"Why don't you just meet up with Tod and have a conversation," she said. "Can't hurt."

The question hung in the air as we took our seats to watch the Pistons whip the Blazers. I kept glancing over to see if Paul Allen was sitting behind the Trail Blazers bench. I started to entertain the prospect of managing the team, pulling it out of its tailspin.

Why wouldn't I want to meet with the guy who handles Paul Allen's sports ventures? So many possibilities.

After the game I found Sarah and asked: "How do I reach Tod?"

A WEEK OR so later Tod Leiweke and I met for dinner at El Gaucho, a steakhouse in the Benson Hotel. Great food, white tablecloths, cigar bar. Born in St. Louis, he had built a solid reputation as an honest dealer running sports franchises, mostly in the northwest. We were supposed to talk over drinks. We knew a ton of the same people. We wound up staying for dinner and closing out El Gaucho four hours later. I left feeling intrigued. The Blazers weren't great. Matter of fact, the franchise was jammed with headaches, from troubled players to dropping attendance. But I also saw plenty of potential to rebuild it into a thriving franchise, starting with the top pick in the upcoming draft.

Tod called the next day. "Good times," he said. "Let's keep in touch."

While they sorted out other candidates, Tod and I met a few more times. Then he called and said: "Okay, Paul wants to meet you."

I'm thinking: "Do I want to meet Paul?" Word was beginning to seep over to Nike that I was in play to take over as the Trail Blazers' president. Talking to Paul Allen would take it to another level.

In the end, I figured, why not? I had little to lose, right? If nothing else, we might develop a new sponsor.

I decided to drive the three hours due north to Seattle to meet with the legendary cofounder of Microsoft, an entrepreneur who might have been worth north of $15 billion at the time. On the way up, as I reached Seattle's radio zone, I tuned into the sports talk station just as the host asked: "What's this about Paul Allen selling the Trail Blazers and the Rose Garden?"

PAUL ALLEN HAD become a billionaire at thirty-three. Two years later, in 1988, he bought the Blazers for $70 million. The Seahawks were threatening to leave Seattle in 1997 when Paul swooped in, bought the team, and became a hometown hero.

Now, still based in Seattle, he had built a reputation as a gener-ous philanthropist but also as a very private man. Like his buddy Bill Gates, Paul Allen rarely flashed his wealth. If anything, he was equally unassuming and disarming.

Paul invited me to his office, minimally furnished and sim-ple. We were alone. No Tod, no staff. He did not call me in to pass the time or engage in small talk. It quickly occurred to me that he considered me the prime candidate. In an ironic way, it reminded me of my interview with the Arthur Andersen re-cruiter who was about to hire me back in 1982—until I owned up to my prison time.

With Paul Allen, I had a different point to make.

"Paul," I said when we got beyond pleasantries, "I'm will-ing to consider making a commitment and leaving my job. It's a good job, but I am willing to leave that. But before I commit to you, I need to know you are committed to this team."

He knew that news had leaked about his intention to sell the Blazers. I can't say he was surprised by my concern. No one in the NBA would have been shocked if Paul unloaded the team. It had the lowest attendance in the league in 2006. He'd lost con-trol of the Rose Garden arena. Why keep the Jail Blazers?

"Here's what happened," he said. In his awkward way, he leaned over his desk and looked me in the eye. "We had nego-tiated a deal for me to sell the team. And the arena. We had it all worked out. I went to bed one night and couldn't sleep. It just kept bothering me. I realized I loved the team, loved being an owner, loved owning the arena. I got up that morning and told my people I wasn't selling the team."

"So, Larry," he said, "I am recommitted."

I saw that Paul Allen was a fan, pure and simple. He was in the process of buying back the arena. And the Trail Blazers had done well in the 2006 draft, trading difficult players and dealing for LaMarcus Aldridge and Brandon Roy. Paul convinced me he wasn't going anywhere.

It was a good conversation, but nothing was offered or decided. Paul had other candidates to consider but kept checking up on me. Tod called me up for a second meeting, this time with Paul's younger sister, Jody, who was deeply involved in Vulcan and all the sports franchises. The meeting went well. Then I met with Paul and Jody together. It felt like a final audition.

I'm sure Paul Allen called David Stern to check on me. David and I were tight. The NBA commissioner was one of the straightest shooters I had ever known. He was in favor of my coming into the league. Same with his number two, Adam Silver. I'm sure David gave Paul the thumbs-up.

Before I got back to my hotel, Tod called. "Hey, Paul wants to close this right now," he said. "Are you in?"

WAS I UP for the super-charged media and security scrutiny that I would inevitably have to face? That was a question that the average prospective candidate might not have to fear. But for an executive harboring a secret life of crime and prison, it was major.

It was one thing to rise through the corporate world without having my secret exposed. Even I was surprised by how much was done with a handshake, a solid network of support and trust.

The chances of my secret coming out if I remained with Nike were slim, but they rose considerably if I made this next move to professional sports.

The NBA is notoriously committed to matters of security, from keeping arenas safe to making sure the franchises are clear and clean.

In addition, my prospective new boss, Paul Allen, was known for being paranoid and worried about optics. Between the background check I had anticipated from the NBA and Allen's internal investigation, I would have expected to be found out.

And if I became team president, the whole world could see me courtside sitting next to Paul Allen. People from my neighborhood and my gang, cellmates, cops, judges.

I weighed the alternatives. But I was thinking: no.

AT NIKE AND Jordan Brand my private interviews became public. Word had gotten out. Inside Nike, the pressure for me to stay was intense. But I listened to other voices.

I fielded a call from Fred Whitfield, then president of the Charlotte Hornets.

"Man," he said, "I heard you were up for the president's job with the Trail Blazers."

Fred and I had become good friends. He was one of the first African-American presidents of an NBA franchise. Fred was one of a few who firmly believed I should take Paul Allen's offer.

He said: "You better take that job." He fully understood the historical significance of a Black person in such a powerful position.

Feeling pressed from both sides, I had only a weekend to decide whether to stay with Jordan and Nike—where I was comfortable and challenged—or take on the risk of running an NBA franchise, about which I knew very little.

"You know what you need to do," MJ said when he realized I was on the fence—and I might actually walk. We had been talking all along. "Stay with us. Nike will make it worth your while. You know what to do."

Actually, I didn't know what to do.

NO NIGHTMARES SATURDAY night, even though I feared the intense public scrutiny that would come with a high-profile role in the NBA. Sunday, I woke up alone and still undecided. I had to go up or down Monday.

I needed to get out of town, away from cell phones and TV. To clear my head, I had often gone to Bonneville Hot Springs, a spa about an hour's drive east into the mountains along the Columbia River. I would soak in the hot springs, get a massage, decompress. Seemed like the perfect place to seek resolution. I hopped in the car, headed into the Cascades, and didn't tell a soul.

Two hours later, I was soaking in the mineral hot springs. My mind indeed was starting to clear, and I saw myself staying with Nike. The thought gave me comfort. There was less risk and more guaranteed upside with Nike. I closed my eyes, secure in my decision. My mind drifted. I took a deep breath of steam rising from the mineral water and begin to relax. I almost fell asleep.

Then this image popped into my head: I always had this picture on the wall in my office of Jackie Robinson on his first day with the Brooklyn Dodgers. He's walking into the locker room for the first time with number 42 on his jersey. He's opening the door and crossing the threshold and breaking the color barrier in Major League Baseball. And with that, he changed everything.

I opened my eyes to make sure I was still at the spa. I closed them and the image reappeared. Jackie with that blue number 42. I tried to regain that sense of peace, but it was gone.

Up to that moment I had been considering the move to the Trail Blazers almost purely in business and lifestyle terms. More money, more control, new challenges—maybe more fun.

Now I considered an added dimension: an opportunity to open a door for people who look like me, for young kids to say, "Wow, if he can do it, I can do it." There were only thirty of these jobs in the world. Maybe there are one or two Black people in those positions, Whitfield being one. I'm not trying to put myself on a Jackie Robinson scale, but this was an opportunity to see if I could succeed in a space where few Blacks have had the opportunity.

Seeing my decision with fresh eyes, I realized I didn't have a choice. There were few Black people in high-profile executive leadership positions, especially in Portland, Oregon. I started to look at my choice as an opportunity I had been blessed with—to not just take this job but to also show that we could do this, too.

I made the long ride down from the mountains, at peace with my decision. Then I let people know.

David Stern called with congratulations.

"Good move," he said. "Whatever you need, I'm here."

Phil Knight was more mindful when I showed up for the second time to tell him I was leaving Nike.

"I get it this time," he said. "We have an okay relationship with the Trail Blazers. With you up there we will have a great one."

12

BLAZING NEW TRAILS

*B*efore I signed my deal with the Trail Blazers, I presented Paul Allen, via Tod Leiweke, with one condition: "I want to be president *and* I want the GM to report to me.

"That's the straightest path to bring us back," I told Tod.

My request was unusual for NBA franchises. Most had a president who handled the business side and was responsible for ticket revenue, sales and advertising, sponsorships, managing up to the owners; then there was a general manager who ran the basketball side: the team, the coach, the players, the draft, the trades. In most franchises there's little connection, planning, or strategy, let alone execution, between the two sides.

That was the only way I was going to sign a seven-year contract to revive a failing franchise. My thinking was, the best possible way to set the franchise up for success was to have the two sides working in concert, so that the businesspeople understood the challenges that faced the team, and the team appreciated that the businesspeople had to do their job. Basic cooperation—teamwork. I saw this as being necessary for the team to be successful.

Tod checked with Paul and Jody. They blessed my dual role, and I took control of the franchise. Kevin Pritchard was GM at the time. He loved the media, which took a ton of pressure off me. That offered some relief.

Sounded good, but what would happen when I tried to put my plan into practice?

Early on I decided to take my leadership team on an off-site session to Miraval, a spa and retreat outside of Tucson. I wanted to work on some team-building stuff, develop some strategies, begin actually working together. But I also made it mandatory for the general manager, his assistant, and the coach to join us from the basketball side.

Nate McMillan was our coach. A few days before the Miraval trip he popped his head in my office.

"So, boss," he said, "you really want me to come?"

"Nate," I responded, "I really need you to be there. It's not a choice."

"All right, all right," he said.

I heard that the GM and some others were griping about being forced to hang with the business side. They changed their tune once they got to Miraval, which is a very luxurious resort, to say the least. It wasn't that complicated, really. We got to know one another, beyond the job, but we also broke down some boundaries around utilizing the players to market the brand in the community. Instead of doing a practice one day, we would need a player or two to attend an event in the community, at a school or playground or somewhere. The coaches had to be on the same page.

The basketball guys not only got it, but they thanked me for inviting them. "One of the best things we've ever done with the franchise," Pritchard told me.

The retreat was the beginning of the franchise's rebound. I had inherited a strong management team that helped get me up to speed on the basics. Instead of selling apparel, we were getting revenue from ticket sales, advertising, merchandising, sponsorships, and TV deals.

I had high hopes for our first pick in the 2007 draft, Greg Oden, a strong, seven-footer with a ton of promise. But Greg got hurt and didn't work out. We could have drafted Kevin Durant. Chalk that up as a massive fail. But it did signal to our fans that the Trail Blazers were serious about putting a solid team on the floor. We traded Zach Randolph, another sign that we were looking for a fresh start.

Paul Allen was in on the Zach Randolph call. He liked Zach, and Zach was a great player, a future Hall of Famer even, but he tended to surround himself with some bad people.

"We're doing this?" Paul asked. I think he expected me alone to weigh in and tell him what we needed to do. The GM, Nate, and I had talked it over and agreed on it together. That put me in the position of suggesting it on the call, and our response to Paul was: "Yeah, we're doing this." As a team.

We were telling the fans that from now on we were not going to just look at bringing in players who were great on the court, but we wanted them to be great people off the court. We brought on players like LaMarcus Aldridge and Brandon Roy. We would sign Juwan Howard to a free agent contract in 2009, another signal that we were bringing on solid citizens and hardworking players. The city responded. Fans started coming back to the Rose Garden. We began selling out the nineteen thousand seats every game.

Before every Blazers home game in my first year, I would walk the concourse, just to talk to fans and answer questions. I considered it part of our marketing, just like getting our players out into the community. We needed the team to become part of Portland. A guy stopped me on the concourse at halftime.

"I've had season tickets for years," he said, "but we stopped coming to the games. I didn't want my nine- and ten-year-old kids coming to the games and looking up to the kind of players on the court. I would give the tickets away.

"Now we're back, and I appreciate everything you've done," he said. "Me and my kids are at every game."

WHAT I WORRIED about in my very public role and on my trips down the concourse was that tap on the shoulder with a tug back to my past. The Trail Blazers job was the scariest for me. All the publicity and media attention was driving me crazy.

Sure enough, one night I was walking along the concourse before tip-off for a Lakers game, and this guy tapped me on the shoulder. A cold chill ran up my neck.

"What's up, Prez?" he said.

It was a friend I'd known for many years from the corporate world. He'd worked in the Clinton White House and would go on to a successful career in the D.C. lobbying world. I relaxed— for a sec.

"I've been hearing from this guy George Hill, who says he knows you from Philly."

George Hill had been one of my friends coming up. He'd been a member of the Cedar Avenue gang, but he never got arrested and he joined the military. By the time I went back to jail, George was out of the military and had joined the Philadelphia sheriff's department. He had boxed, so when we put on boxing matches at Graterford State Penitentiary, George would come up and referee. He would always bring me something from home, usually desserts and treats.

"Yeah, what's George got to say for himself?" I asked.

"He's telling me how proud he is of you, all the stuff you have been through. He does go into some detail."

My stomach dropped.

"Like what?" I asked.

"Like some of the trouble you got into and how he used to visit you when you went away. But he's mostly saying how proud he is, like he knew you when. It's more bragging than malicious."

At this point I clammed up, nodded, and stared. My friend looked around and said: "You need to tell your boy to chill. I'm good, you know, but other people might not take it the right way. Y'know what I mean?"

I knew too well.

I thanked him and prepared to call George the next day. We'd stayed in touch and still spoke from time to time. On the call, we traded news about friends back home before I got down to business.

"I know you're proud of me," I said, "but I need to keep things quiet. Cool?"

Then I straight up asked him to not mention me and those days to anyone, even if he thought they might already know.

"All right," he said. "I'm cool."

I was not. The whole thing rattled me.

That night it all came racing back in a dream that replayed someone tapping me on the shoulder—but the guy tapping me was a cop. The dream went downhill from there, with me getting cuffed in front of fans and walked to the paddy wagon they used to load us into back in Philly.

I woke up relieved the dream had ended, but I was more scared than ever that my secret was about to get out, the house would come down, and the *Portland Oregonian* headline would read: "Jail Blazers Run by a Jailbird."

I spent the rest of the night staring at the ceiling.

THE NBA OWNERS meetings were always interesting. Paul Allen rarely felt motivated to fly to New York and meet with the other owners, so I often found myself sitting at a table surrounded by a bunch of white billionaires. David Stern ran the meetings as if he were back serving sandwiches at his father's deli in the Chelsea section of New York City. He had no problem dropping f-bombs on those boys if they got out of line. I didn't say much, but I was always laughing to myself. I loved Stern.

Stern would occasionally stand up and say: "Everybody out but the owners." The "staff," as in presidents like myself, would push back our chairs, get up, and leave. He would point at me—"Not you"—and I would keep my seat, often the only brother in the room.

Until Michael Jordan showed up at the table.

In early 2010, MJ started negotiating to buy the Charlotte Bobcats. Besides raising the $275 million to become the majority owner, he had to get past the NBA owners. To pass judgment on Jordan's worthiness to join the upper ranks of sports moguls, Stern assembled a committee of owners, primarily the labor committee, to evaluate his record. Since I was a labor committee member, that put me in the position of voting on MJ's admission to the club: Mark Cuban, Jeanie Buss, seven other owners—and me.

MJ and I had remained close after I left Nike. We would check in with each other often. I might see him at a game. We would hang out during the all-star weekends. We had a friendship that went beyond business. He would always tell me, "You'll be back."

So, there I was, sitting across the table from MJ the day he came in for his interview in front of the owners committee. Stern had already circulated the NBA's dossier and research on Michael Jordan's background and net worth. Since I had run his division at Nike for years, I had a sense of the value of his holdings. But the irony of the guy who worked for him now sitting in judgment was not lost on either of us.

Of course, MJ's admission to the NBA club was a sure thing. His net worth was higher than some of the owners. He remained the most famous and well-regarded pro basketball player of all time. There was no way they would reject him. Still, he had to show up and answer questions, most of them fawning.

I didn't say a word during the interview, but I did send him a text afterward: "You killed it, my brother."

FOR THE NEXT two years Jordan and I would show up for the quarterly NBA owners meetings in New York—two Black men among the white billionaires, one from the swampy cropland and tobacco fields of rural North Carolina, one from the rough and rugged streets of West Philly. I would often look around that gathering and ask myself: "How did I get here?"

The whole world knew how Michael Jordan got to the table. He had earned it through raw talent, hard work, unrelenting competitive drive—and Nike.

What about me? Hard work, for sure. Drive to sell, from an early age—absolutely. When I decided to take advantage of the opportunities for education release offered at Graterford State Penitentiary, I was all in and dedicated myself to academic excellence. I developed a single-minded focus on high achievement. I competed to succeed. In that compulsion to succeed and win, Jordan and I were similar. But I brought a sensibility to corporate conference tables—whether at Jantzen, Nike, or the NBA—that not even MJ could match. I showed up with my life lessons from the streets and prison. If I came across as cool at a marketing meeting, it was because I came with a different perspective.

"You know what?" I might be thinking to myself. "There's no gun to my head. I am not standing before a judge who's about to determine my jail term. I don't have to clock into prison before my 8 P.M. curfew."

My panic threshold was very high.

That connection to the streets and Black pro basketball players combined to give me a unique perspective at the NBA owners meetings. Coming up in West Philly, we would see 76ers in the community. Julius Erving would drive through our streets, especially during the 1983 season when he led the team to the world championship. Same with Maurice Cheeks. When "Mo" played point guard for the Sixers from 1978 to 1989, he was a hero in our streets. At Nike and then with the Blazers, I grew close to plenty of players, especially Ray Allen, Carmelo Anthony, Chris Paul, Brandon Roy, Charles Barkley, and many others who became close friends.

All of which made my personal bond with MJ that much deeper and lasting. We would often leave the NBA meetings at the Four Seasons in midtown, slide out the back exit, and walk across the street to have dinner at Lavo, an Italian grill. We traded stories about family and running an NBA franchise. We would discuss what had gone on in the meeting, a couple of friends getting together after work. Every session ended with MJ updating me on the situation with Jordan Brand at Nike and a question about my next move, closing with his familiar admonition: "You'll be back."

THERE WAS NO going back from the pressures of running the Blazers.

I was kicking back one night in March 2012, at my condo in La Jolla, when the phone rang. I'd been watching the Blazers on

TV. The phone rang just as the final horn sounded. Never good. It was our power forward LaMarcus Aldridge. He and I were tight, and although he didn't call me often, on occasion he would reach out.

"Hey, Larry," he said, "I've just gotta tell you something. Nate has lost the team. They're not listening to him anymore."

Not that shocking, considering what I had just seen on TV. The New York Knicks had humiliated the Blazers 121 to 79. It was hard to watch. Our team had lost seven of its last nine games. A promising season had turned to dust. Not only did we have to let Greg Oden go due to injuries, but it seemed like half the players were sitting on the bench in civilian clothes because of injuries. In public, many of the players defended Nate, but even he could see his hold on the locker room was shaky.

"Nate's been the only coach I've had," LaMarcus said, "but other guys on the team are not with him." I sensed that he was speaking on behalf of all the players.

Paul Allen and I had been concerned about Nate's ability to control the players. We had begun to consider letting him go, even though he was still in the first year of a four-year deal. I called Paul and told him what LaMarcus had to say. That was it. We needed to fire Nate.

We had let the general manager Kevin Pritchard go in June 2010, as well, so it was on me to deal with Nate and the media. A few days later, after we got organized, I called Nate.

"Bad news," I said. "I just talked to Paul, and we've decided we're going to go in a different direction . . ."

"Whoa, wait a second," Nate said. "What are you saying?"

Truth is, Nate was not all that surprised, but it was still hard to take. Beyond that, I had engineered a soft landing for him. It was a difficult conversation, but he was cool. Firing people is one of the hardest things about management. The people part is always the biggest challenge for me.

Still in La Jolla, I called up to my team in Portland and asked them to handle the media.

"No," they said, "we need you to show up. You have to break this to the media and the fans."

Flights were sold out for the day, so I figured I was off the hook. But Paul Allen chartered a plane to fly me back.

I would have to face the cameras once again. The news was already out.

ACCOMPANYING THE TRAIL Blazers to Philly whenever we played the Philadelphia 76ers was always tense.

I always invited family and friends to the games. The Sixers were always generous and gave me a suite.

One night I was walking down the concourse with one of the Sixers executives. She and I were comparing notes on ticket sales and stuff. The whole time I was keeping an eye on the crowd coming our way, constantly scanning for a familiar face. I needed to keep my two worlds as separate as possible, but I wasn't making it easy on myself.

Then I saw a guy I knew named Rick coming toward me. Rick was from South Philly, and we were in Camp Hill together. He was a bad dude. He'd shot a bunch of people in the South Philly

High School cafeteria. Rick looked good, but he also looked like he was still in the life. I could tell by his style. I liked Rick and wanted to say hey, but that was the last thing I needed. Who knew what he would have had to say to the woman from the Sixers by my side? He might ask the wrong thing or mention stuff from back in the day.

"Oh, shit," I was thinking. My two worlds were about to collide. One of the reasons I could successfully keep them separate was the physical distance between Philly and Portland, between my criminal side and my life as an upstanding business leader. "Oh, shit."

I couldn't look away. We were a few feet away from one another, but Rick didn't see me, or he didn't recognize me in my suit and tie. Or he felt my fear and knew to keep his distance. He passed. I continued back to my suite, said goodbye to the Sixers exec, turned around, and went looking for Rick. I wanted to catch up with an old brother from around the way. I circled the arena, but I couldn't find him. Probably for the best.

BEING THE PUBLIC face of the Blazers had its benefits.

When Barack Obama was running for president in 2008, he campaigned in Portland a few times. I was tight with Reggie Love, his body man, from his basketball days with Duke. Back then Obama was the junior U.S. senator from Illinois, so security wasn't too crazy, and I got to meet him. We also knew some of the same people from Chicago, like Peter Bynoe, a lawyer whom I'd met through MJ. Peter was an early Obama supporter. The first time we met, Barack and I talked politics. The next time he showed up with Michelle.

"Hey, Michelle," he joked, "come on over and meet the guy who's running everything here in Portland. He knows Bynoe. He's tight with Reggie, too." Michelle wrapped me in a hug.

But there were too many low times with the Blazers. By 2012, five years into a seven-year contract, they began to weigh on me.

True, I got a kick out of the fans, but the media stuff started wearing me out. The tension of keeping the secret was killing me. Dreams at night, migraines by day. Bad combination.

I also found myself defending a number of Paul Allen's decisions that I didn't agree with. Paul would call me and say: "We're doing this." I might argue my side, but at the end of the day, it was his team, his money, and he was the boss—but I often found myself defending things that I didn't believe in. That was not okay.

It was not okay the way he dealt with Rich Cho. Rich and I met in Vegas where I was attending a summer league. The Blazers were in need of a general manager. Rich and I met for lunch and wound up discussing basketball and managing teams for four hours. I called Paul.

"I really like this guy Rich Cho," I said. "He could be our guy."

Allen asked if he had a passport. "I'm in Helsinki and want him to fly over here." They spent six or seven hours on Paul's yacht docked in Helsinki.

"This is our guy," Paul told me. "Get it done."

So, I sealed the deal with Rich. Three months later Paul called me into his office.

He wasn't feeling Rich. He said, "He has to go."

"Wait," I responded. "He hasn't even gotten through a full year with us, and he's making close to a million a year. Give him a chance."

"No," Paul said. "He's out."

That put me on the hunt for another general manager. I was interested in Mitch Kupchak, who was general manager with the Lakers. Mitch had a great reputation as an NBA player and a solid one as GM. Under league rules, I had to ask the team for permission to speak with one of its executives about a job. I had gotten close to Jeanie Buss, as we worked together on the NBA owners labor committee. She was the daughter of Jerry Buss, head of the family that owned the team. Jeanie was very involved in management. I reached her by phone.

"Hey, Jeanie," I said, "you know we are looking for a GM. Is it possible to talk to Mitch?"

She said she would discuss it with her father and brother. A few days later she called back with a no.

"I'm not surprised at that," I said.

She paused. I could sense she had something else to say.

"Let me take my Lakers hat off now and put my Phil Jackson's girlfriend hat on," she said. Phil had coached the Lakers after the Bulls but had been out of basketball for a couple of years. They had been dating and would eventually get engaged. "I know you guys are looking for a coach to replace Nate. Phil might be interested. Would you guys have any interest?"

"Hell, yes," I said. "Phil Jackson coming to coach our team? Absolutely."

My head started to spin. I'm thinking ticket sales, sponsorships, draft picks, free agents, championships.

"Well, I'm going to see Phil this weekend," she said. "Let me get back to you in a few days."

She called back on Monday.

"Phil is absolutely interested," she said. "He knows who you guys are and has respect for you and the team." She also admitted she was being a bit selfish. "I want him to stay on the west coast, so this would work out for me."

Knowing Phil would cost us more than we had been paying Nate McMillan, we ran numbers of what we might expect in revenue boosts. The numbers came out very positive. But I wasn't ready to tell Paul Allen until we were on firmer ground, until it was real. Jeanie put me in touch with Jackson's agent. We went back and forth a few times. He assured me Phil Jackson was very interested in coaching the Blazers and wanted to set up some meetings.

At that point I discussed it with Paul. I gave him all the rationales and the numbers. I was selling it hard. Phil Jackson as coach would put Portland on the map. Paul frowned and sat back in his chair.

"Why would Phil Jackson want to come here?" he asked.

"He wants to get back into basketball," I said, "and he likes our franchise."

"This is not a situation like he's been in the past," Allen said, "where he's had Michael Jordan, Scottie Pippen—or Shaq and Kobe."

"I asked his agent about that. Phil thinks that this would be a new situation where he would try and win a championship with a new mix of players."

I could tell Paul was not going for it. We went back and forth for a while. I left that first meeting with at least the sense we could meet with Phil's agent. I tried to get on Paul's schedule. At the end of the day, Paul would not take a meeting with him.

"Paul," I said, "I don't understand why you wouldn't want to at least take a meeting or two."

He kept making excuses. I called off the negotiations before they had begun.

I took the weekend to think it over. I had to call Jeanie Buss and close the loop. She was disappointed. But so was I. If you are about winning and building a successful franchise, why not bring in the best talent? Why, I asked myself, would an owner not want to even meet with a stellar coach like Phil Jackson? Then the answer came to me: For Paul Allen, it wasn't always about winning. But it was always about control. After many of our home games, he would head into the locker room and corner the coach. "Why didn't this guy play?" he might ask. Or: "Why does so and so foul so much?"

I knew Phil Jackson wouldn't put up with that. He would tell any owner: "Get out of my locker room."

Paul Allen knew that, too. He knew he couldn't handle a personality as big and strong as Phil Jackson. Phil comes in, he's the guy, he's the man. Paul was not up for that.

And I was no longer up for being president of the Trail Blazers.

13

UNBURDENING

One morning in 2008, I called my daughter Laila out of a combination of desperation and determination. The night before I had had a particularly tortured dream. Cops cuffed me. A judge threw me in jail, again. I protested, again. The migraines, the dreams, the living two lives—they had to end.

"We need to talk," I said. "I have some stuff to tell you."

Laila had moved to California in 1999. She'd gotten married in 2002, settled down, and started a family. Laila and her three kids were briefly in Atlanta while her husband, Jason, was on a federal law enforcement training mission.

"What's up, Dad?" she asked.

"I'm ready to work on the book," I said. "Let's do this."

BEYOND MY BROTHERS and sisters, Laila, my first child and elder daughter, knows me the longest and the best. She came up in the

West Philadelphia streets, in the arms of my and Pearl's families. After Philly public schools and Howard University, she moved to Harlem and taught middle school before relocating to California where she started a family. Needless to say, I was not a model father. Her mother, Pearl, and I never married. When she was a toddler, I spent four years behind bars. She watched me turn my life around in jail, witnessed my early success in accounting, and celebrated my rise through the sports apparel business and the Blazers.

Our father-daughter story is deep and complex, at times tragic and painful, but ultimately loving, fulfilling—and trusting.

"Dad," she would often say, "you have a story to tell, and people need to hear it."

"Maybe someday," I would respond.

She'd ask me again and again.

"Nah," I said each time. "It's not about me. I don't want any attention."

Nor did I want to relive my younger, violent days and expose my early life of crime to the world.

But over time, the secret had gained too much power over me. It had forced me to live a split-screen life, my two sides occasionally at war, but most often in nerve-rattling coexistence. I had learned to live as two people, but at a great cost.

With Laila, I had the opportunity to stop the secret from corroding me from the inside. I had reached the point where I needed to bring my two lives together. The secret had to die, perhaps by telling my complete story to my daughter, grim details and all. Finally, the reward was greater than the risk.

There was more. From talking to Brother Wazir and many others, I had learned that the opportunities for inmates through

226

education-release programs had withered, especially in state prisons. The Federal Pell Grants that had helped fund my college degree were no longer available. By telling the story of my success, thanks to vigorous education-release programs, perhaps I could help reemphasize these opportunities for inmates. In addition, and maybe even more important to me, was the thought that maybe by sharing my story I could help to inspire someone to try and pursue a life that may seem out of their reach. To show that we are capable of our wildest dreams when given the opportunities to succeed, even if we've made mistakes.

And I trusted Laila.

LAILA WAS SEVEN when I got out of Graterford, where she had visited me with Pearl.

My love life was complicated, to say the least. I had gotten a divorce from Donna. And I had become close to Carol, who had helped guide me through the education-release system. But I loved my little girl, and I wanted to make things right with Pearl. I made sure the three of us spent time together, and it felt right to me. I had asked Pearl to marry me and build a family, but she was hesitant and ultimately resistant. Perhaps she was too proud or too hurt that I had not devoted myself to her earlier, or perhaps she was already struggling with addiction. Pearl declined my offer, and we never lived together.

In the coming years, crack hit our West Philly neighborhood hard. Pearl surrendered to its destructive pull. Pearl's parents, Ethel and Jack, raised Laila, with help from Pearl's sister, Lucille. And, occasionally, Pearl. Though we never married, I sent checks every month to help raise Laila as soon as I was able. I never missed a payment until she left home to go to college.

Meanwhile, I had married Carol, and we moved to the suburbs north of the city and started a family. As I worked my way up the corporate ladder in Campbell's, Kraft, and the newspaper group, my days were a grind with long commutes on either end. While I was navigating the corporate world, Laila was learning to dodge trouble and navigate the pitfalls of growing up in the hood without a father. I made my presence known in her life in the ways that I could. I bought her her first bike and taught her how to ride it. I showed up to birthday parties. As often as possible I would scoop her up and treat her to lunch or dinner. Over time as I succeeded and got bigger paychecks, the meals improved from Burger King to the finest restaurants in the city. I fit into the role of the "Disney Dad," who showed up to spend fun times with a child then left the more difficult, daily child-rearing duties to others.

"My father is like a special guest star in the story of my childhood," Laila told my sisters. "I always feel grateful for his attention."

Laila would visit me, Carol, and the kids in the suburbs. But as she reached her teens, the visits became less frequent. We drifted apart as she was becoming a young woman, when she needed a father the most.

BY 1992, WHEN Laila graduated from Central High School of Philadelphia, Carol and I had moved out to Portland with our two children, Jamal and Amissa. My stepson, Patren, remained on the east coast, preparing to start college in the fall at the University of Maryland Eastern Shore.

Over the next few years, Laila flew out a few times and even joined us for a memorable and fun-filled trip to Mexico, but she was immersed in making her way at Howard University. I was settling the family into a new city three thousand miles from home and trying to shake Jantzen out of its swimwear stagnation. Laila felt out of place in my new home in the far Northwest, about as far from West Philly and the nation's gritty capital as you could get. Both Philadelphia and D.C. were battling waves of violence brought on by crack cocaine. Portland must have seemed like another planet. Plus, as much as I loved and cared for Laila, she was part of a past life on the other coast that I was compelled to compartmentalize.

Still, we talked by phone and attempted to keep in regular contact. I would take every opportunity to show up in Washington, D.C., so I could check out my starving student daughter and treat her to a night on the town, or at least a decent meal a step up from cafeteria food.

On one of those visits in May 1996, Laila met us for a gathering with Carol's family in the D.C. suburbs. She was in her senior year. I could tell she was gaining confidence and ready to strike out on her own. Late that afternoon Laila became violently ill with stomach cramps. We raced her back to her apartment near Howard University campus. Her phone was ringing. It was her aunt Lucille's husband, Uncle Vernon.

"Sweetie," he said, "your mom has passed away. She's gone."

Pearl had been struggling. As a matter of fact, she had always struggled. Laila tried to visit her in Philly as often as possible. Her health continued to deteriorate, and her condition was compounded by her addictions. She had been living on and off at her mother's place in West Philly, just around the corner from Catharine Street. Her sister, Lucille, "Aunt Lu" to Laila, did all she could to help.

Now Laila knew why she had been throwing up all afternoon. She asked how her mother died.

"It was an asthma attack and her heart just gave out," Aunt Lu said. She died of congestive heart failure at forty-one.

Laila drove immediately to Philadelphia to help with funeral arrangements. I flew immediately home to Portland.

Pearl's funeral was a huge outpouring of love from family and friends from all over the city. I did not attend. Of course, I knew about the funeral, who was there, who was not there. I closed it off, with all the feelings that such an event would have stirred up. I couldn't face the facts of Pearl's life, of Laila's place in mine, and how the street life in West Philly that Pearl represented didn't have any place in the new life I had created in Portland.

The result of my inability to show up was that Laila, our daughter, bore the sadness of losing her mother without me. I went back to work and tried to forget, but I had left my daughter feeling abandoned, with lasting wounds.

THROUGH THE NEXT few years, I attempted to keep up my long-distance relationship with Laila, but the wounds festered.

I made sure to attend her graduation from Howard University and celebrated with a brunch for her and all her friends and their families. I was incredibly proud that my daughter had gotten a degree from a historically Black university, especially Howard. When Laila moved to New York after graduation, I visited every time I swung through town, at least a few times a year.

But I knew something wasn't right. She seemed to be holding back, more closed and reserved. I knew something was bothering her. I suspected it was Pearl's passing and my no-show at her funeral, but I wasn't sure. Carol had sensed the unease and had called Laila: "You have to bring it up and break the ice. Your dad won't."

Laila and I liked to meet at Ashford and Simpson's Sugar Bar on the Upper West Side for dinner and music. It had great Southern cooking and live shows. When we sat down for dinner one night in 1998, I could tell something was up. Laila jumped in as soon as we settled into the booth.

"I am really angry with you," she said, "and I have been since my mom died."

She leaned forward and her eyes welled up. My baby daughter had become a lovely young woman, well-spoken, assured, and, I was to discover, very strong willed.

"I know you two had your issues with each other, and I know you didn't care for her," she said, "but you showed you didn't care for me, either. Why didn't you show up for me?"

Truth is I had struggled with it at the time. My younger sister, Florence, had been Pearl's best friend. We had discussed it.

Florence couldn't deal with burying her best friend. But I had a daughter in mourning.

"I owe you an explanation," I said. "And I know this must have been eating at you ever since. It's been bothering me, too.

"I couldn't do it," I told Laila. "I just could not face it, face you, face the whole scene."

"But why not show up for me?" she asked.

"I wanted to be there for you," I said, "but the whole situation brought me too much pain."

That did not satisfy Laila entirely, but at least she knew that I had thought about her on that day, and that I cared for her feelings, even if I couldn't show up. At least she understood that the decision was based on my inability to face up to that part of my life. At least we had surfaced the pain we both shared.

Laila took a deep breath and nodded. I took it as a qualified okay. We were able to make it through dinner.

And we were able to move on, especially when Laila moved to Los Angeles. On a summer break from teaching in New York, she visited friends in L.A. and realized she felt at home in Southern California. She found work and settled down on this coast, but I can't say we grew very close very fast. Months would go by and we wouldn't be in contact.

IN THE SPRING of 2002, I picked up the phone and saw that Laila was on the other end. I had never stopped loving her or thinking about her daily. I wanted to hear her voice.

"Guess what?" she asked. "I'm getting married."

"Guess what?" I responded. "I'm getting divorced."

Carol and I had grown apart, in part from my constant traveling and brutal work hours. Our lifestyles had kept diverging.

No matter how Carol and I parted, no way did I want to lose contact with our children; we vowed to work hard so that our differences didn't prevent us from raising Amissa and Jamal and Patren, together. And we have.

LAILA'S CALL ABOUT getting married broke years of chilliness, if not silence. It reignited our closeness. We began to visit one another. A year or so later, Laila and Jason had their first child, Asali. The first time I held my first grandchild, I was all in.

Even when Laila was immersed in infants and toddlers, she would ask· "Dad—when are you going to do that book?"

"I'm not interested, Not enough time," I kept responding.

For five more years I put her off.

LAILA LOVES THE NBA. She was captivated by my move to the Trail Blazers in 2007.

"Details, *please!*" she said on a call.

I spared her the details of my negotiations with Paul Allen. She knew all about the off-court shenanigans of the Jail Blazers.

"For me, La, it came down to this vision I had of Jackie Robinson," I said.

I told her about my weekend of soul-searching and vacillating that wound up with my vision of Jackie Robinson breaking down color barriers when he walked into the Brooklyn Dodgers dugout, and how that motivated me to take the Blazers job.

"I love that story, Dad," she said. "That should go in your book."

I laughed it off, but Laila did not. She dug in and became more committed to my telling my story. She had just given birth to her second child, Ananda. She started pressing harder than ever for me to start putting down my story.

"I would like to do it," I told her, "but I just don't have the time."

I was, after all, learning how to run an NBA franchise at the time.

"No problem," Laila said. "Tell it to me. I'll write it down."

She never imagined I might take her up on it.

She also had no idea that keeping the secret and living two lives was killing me inside. So, in October 2008, I made the call.

"I'm ready to work on the book," I said.

She said, "Let's get started."

She was ready. I was ready. It was time to talk. We started conversations that grew into weekend sessions every now and then for the next ten years. Laila's babies grew up. I got a place in La Jolla, to be closer to Laila and my grandkids. As we grew closer, I became more comfortable both with who I was at Nike and who I had been back in West Philly, where both Laila and I had come up.

My two lives began to come together.

OUR FIRST SESSION took place in late October 2008, just before Halloween.

Laila and the kids were living for a time in Stone Mountain, Georgia, about twenty minutes outside of Atlanta, at her aunt Lu's house. Lu and Vernon had invited Laila to stay with them while she was pregnant and Jason was away in training for six months. Asali, my first grandchild, was not quite five and had just started kindergarten. Laila's toddler, Ananda, was occupied with everything, including investigating her new brother, JJ (Jason Jr.). The brutally hot and steamy summer had given way to flawless autumn weather. Laila's little ones were fascinated with Halloween.

I was in Portland at the time of that first call. The Blazers were headed into a rough set of games with the Lakers, Spurs, and Phoenix Suns. Even with the heavy schedule, we had reserved time weeks in advance for the call.

"Warith Deen Mohammed is on my mind a lot these days," I said.

Imam W. Deen Mohammed had passed away in September, about a month before, at seventy-four. He'd been my guide in the Islamic faith since my days at Graterford. He passed quietly, just as he had lived much of his life. I was already feeling the void.

"What was it about his teachings that spoke to you?" Laila asked. I could hear Aunt Lu keeping the children busy digging in the garden while we spoke. We talked for over an hour.

"He was a deep and deeply smart man, very articulate and very clear about the fundamental teachings of Islam," I said. "But he was not a showboat. He didn't make it about himself. He was powerful in a quiet way. He was thorough about his belief in Islam and his faith. That spoke to me. It helped me find my own place of calm."

Laila turned out to be the ideal interviewer. She listened well but asked questions to make me go deeper. Jason Jr., her third baby, had just been born in September. He slept in his baby bouncy chair on the kitchen table right next to her laptop while we had our first session. After three babies, Laila was eager to engage intellectually after not working for over a year.

"Y'know, Dad," she said, "you could have hired a professional biographer to do this job, but you didn't—you chose me. The more we talk, the more I realize that I might be absolutely the best person for the job."

"No doubt," I responded.

Then she asked me, "How did adhering to Islam and the teachings of Warith Deen Mohammed mesh with your being a street dude and a gangster?"

"It didn't," I responded. "My time as a gangster was mostly before I discovered W. Deen and began to seriously study the Qur'an. When I was with Mosque 12 and doing stickups for the Nation, I was more into getting money for the Nation than I was interested in studying Islam."

"But how do you square the teachings of Elijah Muhammad in *Message to the Blackman* with dealing drugs to Black people?" she asked.

"I can't," I said. "They do not go together. But at that time we had all bought into the idea that we had to build up and protect the Nation of Islam, even if that meant extorting people like Cody Blue to keep money flowing into the mosque. Looking back, I can't defend what we did. But it made sense at the time. It was part of our survival in the environment we found ourselves in."

I must admit I reveled in recounting the details of my gangster life, even as I faced the hypocrisies. What I couldn't face was telling Laila about killing that boy.

That would have to wait.

I DIDN'T ASK Michael Jordan for much in the way of favors. It was one way I could distinguish myself from every other person MJ encountered.

But I did ask for one: "Could you call my mother on her birthday? She likes watching the NBA, but she adored watching you."

"No problem," MJ said.

Every November 18, Catherine would pick up the phone and Michael Jordan would say: "Hello, Mom. Is it your birthday?"

I would do my best to be there. She would put her hand over the phone, look up, and say: "It's Michael!"

MJ didn't let me down. But I didn't know how many birthday calls were left.

Catherine Miller, my always-loving, determined, resilient mother, began to lose her health battles in her mid-eighties.

The matriarch all the grandkids called Mom-Mom had traveled the world after retiring from her job managing cleaning crews at Philadelphia International Airport. When traveling became too hard on her, she settled down in her place on Osage Avenue and cooked for everyone: my brothers and sisters in the Philly region, the grandkids, and me when I showed up, which I did whenever I was back east. Whenever the Blazers played the 76ers, I got a suite for Mom-Mom at the arena.

She was getting sicker by the month in late 2009. Her diabetes was getting worse. The doctors diagnosed her with stomach cancer. She had moved to an assisted living facility in Delaware, closer to my sisters Theresa and Leen. The calls from my sisters grew urgent the second week of January. Both Laila and I had made plans to fly back to be by her side. I was in Portland when I got the call: Mom was gone. I had just recently returned from Philly. Fortunately, I was able to spend time with her a few days before she passed. I was thankful to have been able to talk to her and say goodbye.

The funeral was in her home church in Wilmington. All of my brothers and sisters were there except for Jerry, who had already passed away in 2002. I found some solace in holding JJ. My first and only grandson had turned one in September. We were both fidgety. Neither of us could sit for long. But he amused me, and I amused him, until it was time for Laila to feed him.

When she took him from my arms, it hit me how alone and vulnerable I felt without a parent in my life.

TWO YEARS PASSED before Laila and I got together for another session.

Laila's three children consumed her time and attention. Matter of fact, though we chatted about our book project, she had quit talking about scheduling the next interview. It was my turn to arrange for a meeting. I wanted to talk.

"Why not fly up to Portland?" I asked.

Laila's youngest, JJ, was just starting preschool.

"I'd love to get away for a weekend," she said. There was the risk she would sleep the whole time and fly back without filling one page in her notebook, but in hopes of making progress, we arranged a few days of father-daughter time.

It was spring of 2011, and we were both eager to be getting back to work on the project, almost as much as Laila was anticipating some uninterrupted sleep. Laila was also looking forward to a few quiet hours to write. The first day we just hung out and caught a Blazers game that night. The next day Laila slept while I went into the office. When I was done, we headed over to Whole Foods to pick up some dinner, so we could talk and eat—our favorite. We held that second session over baked fish and veggies in various forms. We talked for over two hours, her phone exploding with random texts from home the entire time. She ignored them, especially when I described how I shifted from being "the Champ," a trusted student on the safety patrol, to the thorough, "straight-up hood" and a leader of the Cedar Avenue gang.

Laila had known about the armed robberies that got me into Graterford State Penitentiary. Pearl had told her that I had gotten caught robbing grocery stores. But she was unclear about my earlier jail time at Camp Hill.

"What were you officially sent away for?" she asked. I paused. I took in a few breaths and stared at my daughter each time I exhaled.

"Homicide."

There it was. Now it was Laila's turn to take a few breaths and gather herself together. She clearly wasn't ready to learn that her beloved father, the "special guest star in the story of her childhood," had committed murder.

She swallowed her first reaction, which was to blurt out: "What?" She regained her composure as the interviewer, so it came out as: "What happened?"

I told her that we were at a party, and we were all drinking.

"We got into a fight with members of a rival gang that crashed the party," I said. "One thing led to another, knives came out, I wound up shooting a guy. He died."

That was not exactly what happened, but it was close enough for the first time I admitted it to my kid. She looked at me. She began to comprehend. She inhaled down to her toes, put her head down, and kept writing. The she raised her head and caught my eyes again.

"That's a lot. But that's okay."

There was more, as in the real story, of course. But I had to step into that territory carefully. I had to see how it felt to let my daughter know I had killed someone. She wasn't repelled. In that, I felt my first sense of relief.

THE DAY BEFORE Thanksgiving 2011 was another memorable session. I was at Laila's house for the holiday. We always celebrate Thanksgiving at her place. Every year members from both her mother's and my side of the family all meet up at her house and feast. It's glorious! There are always at least twenty of us now, but in the beginning, it was just her little family and me. The anxiety of all that cooking and cleaning hit Laila a few days

240

before, and she was deep in the swing of it when she packed up her recorder and drove down to La Jolla to meet up with me.

That Thanksgiving was particularly stressful for her because it was also the week of Asali's birthday, and her husband decided (against her protests) to get her a puppy for turning eight. They were off picking up the puppy from some breeder while she was in La Jolla with me. As we talked, she was anticipating the chaos awaiting her at home.

We started off our interview on the rooftop deck of my condo. The picturesque ocean view made for a weird contrast with the dark subject matter we discussed. "Let's talk about life behind bars at Graterford," she said.

So, I told stories about me and Brother Wazir, how we watched that inmate deck a corrections officer, how he died on the floor and the inmate would later die in his cell. About racing to class and racing even faster to make curfew. About building the mosque in the prison with Imam Jabbar, one of the most notorious figures in Philly's Black Mafia, who held prayer meetings and allegedly controlled the drug trade inside.

"Incredible stories, Dad," Laila said.

Laila couldn't shake the fact that her father had taken a life. It had happened so long ago, fifty years or so, but that didn't dull the harsh reality.

"Can you tell me more details about that boy who died?" she asked. "What was he like?"

Good question. Could I? Was I prepared to reveal the whole truth? "He was just like me in a lot of ways," I said. "Black boys. Close in age. Hanging out in West Philly."

It was time.

"We were drinking, me and three friends. We wanted to get revenge for one of our young friends who had been killed. We went out looking for someone to make them pay. We found this boy at Fifty-Third and Locust Street, in the heart of the rival gang's territory. And I shot him," I said. "And we went looking for another."

This time Laila stopped writing, stopped recording, stopped asking. She was thinking about JJ. She was the mother of a Black boy. She worried about him and his future every day. She was trying to come to grips with the fact that her father had gone out to kill another Black boy.

"Dad" was all she said.

That was the secret. It wasn't the drug dealing or the armed robberies. It wasn't extortion in the name of the Nation. It was the truth that I had shot another Black boy just like me. There it was. I had made a terrible mistake, and I had served my time, but I hadn't served up the remorse in proportion to the crime. In telling it to Laila, it was as if I were facing up to what I had done for the first time. I had taken a life, and so easily.

Laila didn't ask the questions I was asking myself. It could have been out of respect, or awe, or fear. She held back and came to her own understanding, her own acceptance. That we are not defined by the worst things we have done in our lives. That her father is not the same person he was at sixteen. That we need to have mercy for one another and a hope for redemption, rather than the American way of locking people up forever.

I was asking myself: Why me as opposed to Brother Wazir?

Each of us had taken a life. Why was he still serving a life sentence in Graterford, when his three accomplices had been free for decades? And I had gotten out after less than five years. Wazir was at least as good a man as I, perhaps better. Where was his redemption? When would he finish paying his debt to society?

I had to deal with a different debt—actually a few. One to myself, for cutting off part of my life and making a deal to live two lives. Another debt to the friends and family and loved ones who knew only the half I chose to reveal. Yet another to the people who could have benefited from my sharing the whole of my life, knowing that they could achieve what I had, given the opportunities.

There would be time for paying those debts, especially the last. But starting to tell the truth was slowly beginning to set me free.

14

WHAT TOOK YOU SO LONG?

*I*n the summer of 2015, Charles Woodson called up MJ with some tempting news.

"The University of Michigan is negotiating a new sponsor ship deal with Nike," he said. "But the football team wants to be with Jordan Brand." MJ told him to call me up right away.

Charles and I had been tight for years. He had played for the Wolverines' national championship team in 1997, gone both ways and won the Heisman Trophy, the first and only player to win the trophy while playing offense and defense. He went on to a standout pro career, won a Super Bowl with the Green Bay Packers, and made the Pro Bowl in three different decades. I had brought him on as a Jordan athlete for most of his playing career. He had just retired and signed on with ESPN.

Charles was still very plugged in at his alma mater.

"Wow," I responded. "That's interesting."

And timely. Jordan and I were eager for an opportunity to break out of college basketball and into other NCAA sports—starting with football. Jim Harbaugh was returning to his alma mater to coach the Wolverines after a stint with the San Francisco 49ers. Jordan knew Harbaugh. And I knew I was in the right place back with Jordan Brand. It felt like coming home.

NEARLY FOUR YEARS earlier, by 2012, I instinctively felt my time with the Trail Blazers drawing to a close. Being the public face of the Portland franchise was wearing on me. Everybody wanted to tell me how to run the team—waiters, fans, my dry cleaner. In all my years at Nike and Jordan Brand, no one would tell me how to sell shoes. I had helped turn a franchise with falling attendance in 2007—known for players with rap sheets—into an upstanding member of the Portland community with a run of five sellout seasons. Five years as president was enough for me. MJ felt that. We talked all the time. "C'mon back," he would say.

I felt like it was the right time to move on and head back to the Jordan Brand.

It took a few months to work out the details, but I did return in July 2012—as president of Jordan Brand.

When the deal was done, MJ called.

"What took you so long?" he asked.

ONE WAY OUR brand had kept its connection to the street was the Jordan Brand Classic basketball tournament. We had launched the tournament in 2002 to showcase the best high school players in the nation, competing for the tournament championship and top MVP honors. Amar'e Stoudemire had won that first year, LeBron James the next, then Dwight Howard and Kevin Durant in 2006. On my return in 2012, Julius Randle had just won MVP honors, but the arena was half empty, and only a few of the best high school players bothered to show up. Media ignored it.

Why had the tournament lost its appeal? For years it had been played at Madison Square Garden, but when MJ bought the Charlotte Hornets, he had moved the games to the city's Time Warner Cable Arena. Not so cool. I had a better idea and called MJ.

"Listen, man, I wanted to give you a heads-up," I said. "We need to move the tournament back to New York."

"And why's that?"

"The games aren't resonating with consumers—or the players," I explained. "It's dropped off the scene. Nobody cares about it. Let's try it back in New York."

After some more back-and-forth, he signed off.

"Cool," he said.

Next, I called Charlotte's president, my buddy Fred Whitfield, and explained my reason for wanting to move the games out of Charlotte. He agreed.

But Madison Square Garden was under construction. The Brooklyn Nets were the new, hot team in New York, and their Barclay Center was the new, hip venue. I wired up the move to Brooklyn, and we held the 2013 Jordan Brand Classic at the Barclay Center. I was able to showcase my friends Spike Lee and Carmelo Anthony, Yankees pitcher C.C. Sabathia, LaLa

Vasquez Anthony, and more. Andrew Wiggins was the star on the court, on his way to NBA rookie-of-the-year honors with the Minnesota Timberwolves. MJ showed up and the crowd jumped to its feet. Drake put on a show after the games. The event was packed.

Black Enterprise said it amounted to "a level of pageantry previously unseen in a high school basketball all-star game."

Jordan Brand was getting its cool back. But it came with a cost—Jordans were so cool and in demand that they had driven some people to violence. In a few cases consumers became violent in the frenzy to purchase the latest release. And on rare occasions, people stole shoes from people and shot them in the process of robbing them.

The fact that rolling out new shoes could lead to violence in a few instances broke my heart.

My team studied the causes and consequences, and we did our best to make the experience of buying shoes more safe and secure. We worked with retailers to reduce potential problems. To dampen scarcity, we literally put more product in the market. We released shoes on weekends rather than school days so no kids would feel compelled to miss class. And when we started building the online sales capabilities, that helped to ease the turmoil at launch.

Still, the violence tears me up.

RESTORING JORDAN BRAND'S quality and connection to the consumer was essential, but if we wanted to grow, we had to begin expanding our market, beginning with colleges.

We had been hoping for a Michigan opportunity, so when

Charles Woodson called in 2015 with the tip that Wolverine football was open to a new sponsor, I jumped on it. If we could get our signature Jumpman logo on Michigan football uniforms and supply their gear, Jordan Brand could open up a whole new market—not just in college, but in the NFL. I quickly found that the competition was intense, the dollars were high, and Michigan was likely to stick with Nike.

The Wolverines had lured Jim Harbaugh from the NFL's San Francisco 49ers starting with the 2015 season. Harbaugh had played quarterback for Michigan back in the day.

When negotiations came to a head, MJ and I were together at an event in Mexico. I put out feelers to find the best way to contact Harbaugh. Through sources I tracked him down before he started his new gig as Michigan coach.

"He's in Europe with his family," I told MJ.

"Let's get on a plane and meet up with him," he said.

There was a more efficient way to get it done. I tracked down his cell phone number through a confidential source.

First try, no answer. Second call gets picked up.

"This is Jim Harbaugh. Who am I speaking to?"

"Hey, Jimmy," MJ said.

"Who's this?"

"This is Michael Jordan."

"*The* Michael Jordan?"

"How many Michael Jordans do you know?"

Jordan made his case for the Wolverine football team going with Jordan Brand. "Anything Nike can do," he said, "we can do better."

Once we got Harbaugh's green light, we were able to

negotiate a great deal that was beneficial to both Jordan Brand and Michigan—and ultimately Nike, since we were both competitive and joined at the hip.

The competition spoke to MJ's core need to win, of course. He relished every opportunity to beat Nike to new products, better revenues, better events—especially at NBA all-star weekend. Over time it had become professional basketball's annual convention. It brought players, coaches, owners, fans, sportswear companies, and the media together in one crazed weekend. Every year Michael Jordan wanted to own the weekend with the best brand and the hottest, most sought-after products and events. We had made the Jordan party on Friday night the place to see and be seen over all other events. But every year we were under pressure to outdo ourselves by stepping up the entertainment.

For the 2004 all-star weekend in L.A., we commissioned a documentary on sneakerheads that we planned to debut at the Jordan party. A week before the game we previewed the first cut. It was awful. We were facing a Jordan party dud. My team got together to fill the void. "Why don't we put on a comedy show?" We invited Steve Harvey, Cedric the Entertainer, Bernie Mac, D.L. Hughley, Mike Epps, and Chris Tucker. They all showed and put on a hilarious performance.

MJ was front and center, and Jordan Brand owned all-star weekend, again.

MJ MIGHT BE loyal to the North Carolina Tar Heels, but when the Wolverines debuted their Jordan Brand gear for the 2016 season,

MJ showed up in Ann Arbor to make sure everyone was happy. "Big house, Big plans," Jordan Brand tweeted. In a two-line video attached to the tweet, Jordan appeared in a white shirt and said: "I want to welcome the first football team into the Jordan family. Go Blue."

Harbaugh tweeted back: "Thanks, MJ. It will be an honor to share the sideline with you."

Once the Michigan deal got done, we signed football sponsorships with the University of North Carolina, then Oklahoma and Florida, with more in the works. We aimed Jordan Brand's expansion into other terrain, both athletic and geographic, across the oceans.

THE OPENING OF our Jordan Bastille shop in Paris in November 2016 was the height of fashion, momentarily. More important, it led to Jumpman soccer.

The year before we had opened our first flagship store in Chicago. Then we broke out internationally to Hong Kong with plans for Toronto and Dubai. Jordan Bastille, at 12 rue du Faubourg Saint-Antoine, was our first venture into Western Europe. Every aspect of the two-story shop was finely designed and detailed, including the Jumpman logo outline in white neon on the ceiling.

I was not new to Paris, but I was new to seeing Air Jordans and Jumpman apparel on what seemed to be every other person on the street. It's safe to say the brand was a hit in the French capital.

At dinner that night Bert Hoyt took me aside. The opening of the Jordan shop had blown away Bert, the head of Nike in Western Europe. And it gave him ideas.

"Are you interested in expanding into soccer?" he asked.

Jordan Brand already had a deal with the French Basketball Federation, so we knew the business terrain.

"Why do you ask?"

"PSG's deal with Nike is about to expire," he said. "Now that you are set up here in Paris, maybe they would be interested in seeing Jumpman on all their gear."

"Tell me what I need to do," I responded, "and we will make it happen."

Paris Saint-Germain was one of the most storied "football" franchises in Europe. Their gear had style, of course, but not Jordan—yet.

Bert called back and said Nike was willing to give up its deal with PSG so that Jordan Brand could break into soccer. We were under the same corporate umbrella, after all, and Nike already had its share of soccer teams.

It wasn't until 2018 that we introduced PSG's inaugural Jordan Brand soccer shoes and apparel, but soccer would prove to be a profitable sport for us. In my first run as Jordan Brand president, we had moved from the hard court to the boxing ring. We had broken into football with Harbaugh and the Wolverines in 2015. And soccer in 2018.

When I came back to Jordan after the Blazers, its annual revenues were hovering above $1 billion. Now they were closer to $3 billion.

TELLING MY STORY to Laila was settling my soul, ending my occasional nighttime horrors. But traveling out of the country still made me nervous, in a way domestic travel did not. Sure, I had my passport and was used to flying all over the globe. But each time I presented it, I wondered if this might be the time the secret slipped out.

"Why don't you get Global Entry?" my assistant asked. "That way you could avoid security lines and breeze through airports."

"What do I need to apply?" I asked.

"Fingerprints," she said. "They scan your fingerprints at these special kiosks at the airport."

Fingerprints? No way. That could be a clear path to the dude with all the felonies.

"I'll pass," I said.

I didn't have to leave Portland to be reminded that the decision to keep my criminal life a secret still put me in a risky position. It always came my way, like the time President Obama came to Nike in the spring of 2015.

In the middle of his efforts to expand global trade through the Trans-Pacific Partnership, Obama chose to deliver a speech at Nike headquarters. That in itself ratcheted up the conflict over the controversial trade deal, since Nike's factories in Vietnam and other countries in Asia turned out the bulk of its footwear. But Obama's visit ratcheted up my anxiety, because I knew I was going to attend his speech and the reception afterward on the Nike campus, and I knew I would connect with him personally.

Once again, I wondered how deeply the FBI or Secret Service would investigate my past and whether it was worth the risk. Once again, I said, "Sure," and told the Nike security folks to put me on the list of invitees. I wanted to show up for the president.

I put my name in for a security clearance on May 1. The president was showing up a week later. I was shaken up all weekend. It was the first time post-9/11 that the Secret Service would be digging into my past. What happens if I am barred from being in a room with the president? Does Phil Knight fire me immediately?

Monday, no word. Tuesday, nothing. Obama was showing up in three days. Midmorning Wednesday I was driving in to the office when I got a call from one of the organizers who I happened to know.

"Hey, umm, the Secret Service ran your name and there was a guy named Larry Miller from Philadelphia who came up with a bunch of felonies and shit. What's your middle name? This guy was Larry G."

I said, "My middle name is Garland."

"Cool, cool," he said. "I'll get back to them. Should be fine. No problem."

I had to pull the car over and just sit with it for a while. He called back.

"We're good," he said. "The other Larry Miller was a bad dude."

When we met, the president and I talked about Jordan Brand and the possibility of adding a basketball court to his presidential library. "So, you're the guy who sends MJ all those fat checks," he said.

And since I had passed his security, I could keep at it.

BY 2018, I was ready to make a change in my work life.

I started at Nike in 1997 and became president of Jordan Brand two years later. Excluding my five years running the Portland Trail Blazers, I had been at Nike for eighteen years. Revenues for the brand were $150 million when I started; now they were close to $4 billion. In the last quarter of 2019, we racked up the brand's first billion-dollar quarter. To say MJ's company was on solid ground was an understatement.

I loved Nike, as much as one could love a massive corporation with all its complications, confusion, inconsistencies, and benefits. It had been my home for nearly two decades. I had grown within it and grown a division that was responsible for more than 8 percent of its revenues. Before I got to Nike in 1997, I had worked at six jobs for five different companies. At Nike I could travel the world making deals with and for the most famous athlete of all time. Why would I want to end that?

One by one Nike's top execs appealed to me to stay at the top. I told everyone I still loved the brand and the work and was willing to keep my hand in—just not at the same pace and pressure. MJ called.

"What about if we create a Jordan Brand advisory board," he asked, "and you get to be chairman?"

I thought it over. Nike gets to keep me in a leadership role and take advantage of my relationships and deal-making style; I get to relinquish responsibility for day-to-day management and operations.

"Let's move in that direction," I responded.

We worked out the details toward the end of 2018. In January 2019, Nike announced my new role as first chair of the newly created advisory board. Craig Williams came over from Coca-Cola to become president. Besides the fact that I had to move my office to a less hectic—meaning less fun—part of the campus, and I was less involved in daily decision-making, my work life was still full and demanding.

TAKE, FOR EXAMPLE, the Zion Williamson deal.

The standout star from Duke entered the NBA 2019 draft after his freshman year. He signed with the New Orleans Pelicans, but which sports apparel company would sign him up to a sponsorship deal? Puma and Adidas were in the running, along with Nike and Jordan Brand. The outlines of the deals being presented to Zion were clear: Some companies, like Puma, were dangling huge dollars. Amounts that would add up to the richest shoe deal ever for a rookie. Zion's advisors were telling him to go for the biggest payday, which wasn't Jordan Brand.

Although I was no longer at the head of Jordan Brand, I recognized the value of landing Zion. He was ideal for Jordan Brand. He is an excellent player on the court and a leader off the court. Barring injury, he is headed for a long career at the top of the NBA and a trip to the Hall of Fame. We needed a young superstar player.

I'd found out from a close friend of mine that Zion wanted to sign with Jordan Brand, but he needed to satisfy his advisors with a sweeter deal. I huddled with H. White, who was instrumental in bringing MJ to Nike back in 1984. Keep in mind, Zion was born two years after MJ played his last game for the Chicago Bulls. H suggested we bring Zion out to the campus for a full-on tour, just as he had done with MJ. We were aware that when MJ was in Zion's position, fresh out of college, he had preferred Adidas, until he came to see the campus.

When Zion came to Portland, we made him feel part of the family. And we came up with a competitive offer.

Working quietly behind the scenes, I had no interest in taking any credit, but I did what I could to help land the top player of the day.

ZION WILLIAMSON IS one of the premier faces of the future Jordan Brand, another indication that we have evolved into a brand that means more than just Michael Jordan, the person. We wanted the brand to represent the excellence that MJ achieved on and off the court. One of our campaigns featured some of our Jordan athletes in conversation, and what they were basically saying was: "I'm not Michael, but I am Jordan," meaning that "I am the gold standard of whatever it is that I do. That is what it means to be Jordan."

There are so many young people out there who never saw

Michael Jordan play but who understand and appreciate his caliber of athleticism. Somebody asked my grandson when he was eight who his favorite basketball player was, and he said Michael Jordan. You might wonder: How in the world can Michael Jordan be his favorite player? *Space Jam* does a lot to assist with that awareness. Kids are still watching it. YouTube is another big factor. Whenever people look him up on YouTube, he never misses. YouTube shows only the highlights, so he's making almost every shot. The miniseries *The Last Dance* introduced MJ to a whole new generation of sports fans. And then there are the shoes.

I went to an L.A. Clippers game and sat by an Asian dad with his family of four, all wearing the latest Jordans that had just been released. The guy I was sitting next to works for the Golden State Warriors. Another guy I know who works for the Clippers came up and we started talking. We all did some introductions, and one says to the other, "This is the president of Jordan."

The dad with the family overheard and asked, "You're the president of Jordan?"

He pulled up a picture of his entire family, about ten or fifteen people, and all of them had posed with a foot in a circle. Every single foot had on a Jordan. He told me that they get every Jordan that comes out. It was amazing.

After the game I was in the back area near the locker rooms, and a Hispanic man came up with his whole family, all wearing Jordans, and he told me how much they love the shoes and how it was an honor to meet me. It's come a long way from being just about Michael Jordan, although it still is about Michael to a large degree, since he is where it all originates from. The brand is what he did and what he represents, but it has become bigger than that at this point, and it's continuing to grow.

Jordan is truly a global brand. We are now growing outside the U.S. at a faster pace than we're growing domestically, especially in China and Europe. When I used to go to Europe before, we couldn't get the time of day. They were all about running and soccer. That was all they wanted to hear about from a business perspective. Now, basketball is starting to get some traction, but it's really Jordan that's doing it. We're leading the market when it comes to basketball and sportswear, and growing. It has reached global status and building even more so.

And I think we've only scratched the surface. We're going to get further into women's merchandise. I think there is the opportunity for us to be in every sport, just like Nike. We just have to continue to build on it.

AT 9 A.M. ON a Friday morning in December 2019, I was in the front row of a courtroom in Harrisburg, the Pennsylvania capital, to attend the commutation hearing for my friend Brother Wazir. He had spent more than fifty years in Graterford State Penitentiary, using the time to learn, teach, mentor, farm, and pray. He had even managed the difficult task of parenting his three daughters from inside, and they love him dearly.

Over the decades since my release in 1900, I visited as often as possible. I rarely missed a chance to make it to Graterford when

I was back east. Wazir and I had stayed in touch by phone and email. I never gave up.

In 2017, my politically connected friend Fareed Ahmed came on as an ally in gaining commutation for Wazir. Fareed had connections in the capital city, legislature, and executive branch of Pennsylvania that helped.

All five members of the commutation board have to vote unanimously to commute an inmate's sentence. The process is laborious and tedious. Wazir had been through it all countless times, and the results varied over the years. The last time he lost 0–5 and had all but given up.

But Fareed believed Wazir should be free and had been lining up support behind the scenes. Attorney General of Pennsylvania Josh Shapiro was generally against commutation and had previously voted against Wazir. Fareed convinced Edward Rendell—former Philadelphia mayor and a two-term Pennsylvania governor—to help change Shapiro's mind.

Wazir didn't see any hope in applying, but Fareed convinced him to appeal one more time, which put me in that courtroom. There were nine inmates up for commutation. Wazir had already appeared before the board the day before. I was there for the vote. The board voted down the first appeal. Wazir was second. I watched as each board member gave a thumbs-up, with Shapiro the final vote. He approved, and Wazir was on the road to freedom—the only one of nine to make it that day.

Wazir was already on a bus back to prison. When he arrived, the warden said: "Start packing up your stuff. You're getting out of here." He could not believe his ears.

Wazir and I spoke later that day. He was measured, even solemn, for good reason: nothing is easy or simple in getting released from jail, as we were to find out. Months later, long into 2020, even with the commutation board's vote to commute his sentence, Wazir was still in prison. It usually took ninety days to process papers and arrange the release, but with confusion caused by COVID-19 and bureaucratic delays, it was going on six months before Wazir called.

"The governor finally signed my release," he said.

I was at home in Portland. My friend would be free in a few days, after fifty-two years in prison. No way would I miss that. Despite concerns about getting exposed to the virus, I hopped on a plane to Philadelphia so I could be there when he took his first step beyond the walls. We joined up at a halfway house on Callowhill Street in North Philly.

"Look, there's the skyline I've been seeing on TV every day," he said. "There it is in real life."

In real life, out of his prison garb, Brother Wazir looked relaxed in jeans and a T-shirt, surrounded by his daughters. It started to rain. He spread his hands out and looked up to face the drops.

"This is good," he said. "It's not penitentiary rain."

We drove around Philly and did Philly things. He wanted an all-beef hot dog at the Reading Terminal. He wanted Rita's water ice on South Street. We grabbed a meal at a diner in South Philly.

In the coming weeks Wazir found work at the Sister Clara Mohammad School at the mosque on Wyalusing Avenue in

North Philly. He reunited with his brother whom he hadn't seen in fifty-two years. He settled into life surrounded by his daughters and soon after married the mother of his two youngest.

"The king is back on his throne" was their line.

Wazir's freedom fulfilled a promise I had made to him—and to myself—four decades earlier. It gave me a deep sense of fulfillment beyond anything I had accomplished in the business game. Wazir was a free man.

15

COMMUNITY CALLS

*I*n the fall of 2015, a few weeks after the start of the school year, I stopped by the Little Black Pearl on Chicago's South Side. Monica Haslip, who had founded the high school focused on art, greeted me.

"How's it going today?" I asked.

"Well," she said, "it's been an interesting day."

Monica is an Alabama native with art school degrees. After a career in publishing and media, she started an after-school program in 1994 out of her house on Chicago's South Side. She expanded into a new building for her community-based art and education center, which she transformed into a charter high school. In 2013, Monica's Little Black Pearl Art and Design Academy joined the Chicago Public Schools system. It trains students in visual arts, photography, sculpture, glass blowing, and other creative enterprises.

"Really," I responded. "Interesting how? Good or bad?"

"Interesting bad—one of our kids was killed over the weekend."

Jordan Brand vice president Howard White and I had visited Monica a few months earlier. We talked to the students about how we'd gotten into business as a way to motivate them and build direct lines between the company and the community. Starting in this small Chicago school, me and H were on a mission to use Jordan Brand to support educational programs around the country.

"You know, the kids are pretty upset," Monica said. "It's been a really crazy day. We're about to gather together about twenty of our most influential boys. Would you mind talking to them?"

This was maybe around ten or eleven o'clock in the morning. I could feel the tension in the building. There was extra security all around the school. I thought to myself that maybe I should come back another day. Maybe this was not the right day for me to be there. I was hoping to see how the school functioned on a "normal" day, not one inundated in grief and crisis.

"Give me a sec," I said.

I thought for a minute and asked myself: What's "normal" for kids living in a place like Chicago's South Side and my coming up in West Philly? It's a sad fact that homicides are their normal.

I returned to Monica's office. "Sure," I said.

We came together in a large classroom, me and about twenty students. I can't say they looked overjoyed to be in a room with an older Black guy in a suit and tie. Some looked angry, others ready to be bored, most seemed distracted—for obvious reasons. I sat down in a chair, caught as many eyes as possible, and started in.

"I was you many years ago," I said.

I talked about coming up in the hood in Philly. I described what I do and how I got to Jordan Brand. At first, they were hardly engaging or asking any questions. Then the Jordan thing got them going. They started asking about shoes, my job, what kind of car I drive, and things like that. I don't mind sharing that stuff with kids. "Yeah," I told them, "and you can do the same thing—yeah, I drive a nice car and so can you."

I ached to tell them the whole Larry Miller story, including the gangster who served time, the felon who made it out. But maintaining the secret kept me from sharing that part of myself, and that hurt. It always hurt. I wanted to come clean.

Then one of the Little Black Pearl students took it in a different direction.

"We've been trying to get Ms. Monica to let us have a basketball team here," he said. "Can you help us get that?"

The school didn't have a gym, but the students were using one in a building nearby. School counselors had offered to coach.

"You know what?" I said. "If Ms. Monica lets you guys have a team, I'll gear the whole team up."

As I flew from Chicago to Philly for meetings, I kept thinking about those kids at Little Black Pearl. I was them. They were me. Why did I survive and thrive? And how could I improve their chances for success?

Instead of driving directly from the airport to my hotel, I

decided to weave through the old neighborhood, past the tiny row house on Catharine Street where I grew up, down Baltimore Avenue and across Fifty-Second Street. I saw all the old corners and blocks I used to walk and hang out on every day. Sadly, many looked the same way they did forty years ago. Little row houses were collapsing from within. People looked down and out. I wondered: "Why am I not still here? Why am I not standing on these corners? How did I get from here to what I'm doing today? Why am I walking around the Nike campus all week instead of wasting away in the penitentiary yard at Graterford?"

When I think back now on all of it, the best thing that ever happened to me was getting busted that last time and going to jail. But I would never have chosen to do that, right? I would never have said: "Yeah, I think I'll go to jail." But it led to everything else that I've been able to do with my life. I also avoided so much of the violence that bloodied Philly streets among people I was associated with. And I avoided getting drafted to serve in the Vietnam War. But I never would have said: "I think I'll rob some spots, then I'll get caught and go to jail, but from there, everything's gonna be all right!"

I think of all the other brothers who were incarcerated with me. I think of Wazir. He didn't do anything any worse than I did. I think of all the other brothers who were there with me who are still in prison. I could have gotten a life sentence and still be serving time and never gotten out. Or, I could have gotten fifty years for armed robbery and still be behind bars.

I don't feel the need to fully answer the question "Why me?"

266

That's impossible. But I know there's got to be a purpose for it. This is all too much for it just to be random. This didn't just happen.

Nor do I feel an overwhelming need to share the story of my secret past with the world. The only reason for me to narrate my life is that hopefully my story can inspire somebody who either is down and out and can't see a way out, or young people who are in a rough environment and all they can see is what's going on around them. To me, it's about conveying a message that a person can come up out of that stuff and end up doing some pretty amazing things. I want to open up options and opportunities for folks—offer hope.

I'm no different from anybody else. I was just fortunate enough to have the opportunity to go to school and the smarts and ambition to seize that opportunity. I had some things fall into place that helped me get over the hurdles. The rest was just working hard and being aware. And I know that using my street smarts helped a lot in the whole corporate scene. After all, back in the day I was Air Jordan's target consumer—a leader on the streets.

I am on a mission to highlight the need to reinstate education-release programs. We must increase options and preparation for incarcerated people when they are behind bars so they can succeed on the outside. And along the way, we can start to rethink our treatment and perception of those who have been previously incarcerated. Without the stigma that is attached to having served time, maybe I would not have felt the need to keep my secret for as long as I have.

Maybe that's why I'm not still standing on a corner on

Baltimore Avenue or attending the mosque inside Graterford. And why I found myself at Little Black Pearl that day.

A DAY LATER, Monica Haslip called me from Little Black Pearl.

"You don't even know," she said. "These kids are so excited!"

The kids had put together a petition asking her to okay their having a basketball team that practiced and played in the school. She knew they were about to move into a new space that could be built out with a gym, so she approved the team.

"You gave these boys hope," she said. We followed through and gave them Jordan Brand gear, for starters.

I didn't show up at Monica's South Side Chicago school on an impulse. I always looked for ways to work with kids, starting with the mentoring organization that Saleem connected me to while I was taking classes at Temple and still in the halfway house. As soon as I started at Campbell's, I joined Junior Achievement and gave classes at the middle school on Germantown Avenue. When I settled into Portland and started to work at Jantzen, I hooked up with Tony Hopson at Self Enhancement, Inc. That began a twenty-five-year commitment. I always wanted to do more.

Our relationship with Little Black Pearl grew beyond the court. We helped them develop clothing and shoe design classes at the high school. We brought students out to the Nike campus to work directly with shoe and clothing designers. They toured the University of Oregon campus. Their worlds expanded.

Clearly, we were onto a winning combination: Jordan Brand,

shoes, design, education, motivation. It was time to play it out for students nationwide, beginning where I began.

WEST PHILADELPHIA HIGH School was built in 1912 and occupied an entire block along Walnut Street and Forty-Seventh Street when I was coming up. The first time I stepped into West Philly High it was in the new building along Chestnut Street at Forty-Ninth, not quite as enormous and grand as the original structure, but the perfect place to roll out our latest attempt to use Jordan gear to inspire students.

"I grew up a few blocks away from here on Catharine Street," I told an audience of mostly Black high school kids. "Now I am president of Jordan Brand, and we have an offer for you."

Then I rolled out the basics: if they received good grades, they could turn them into points that they could apply toward buying Jordan products at a local sporting goods store.

"We're calling it 'As for Js,'" I said. "You achieve As and we will make it easier to get Jordan shoes and gear."

A lot of kids want the product but don't have the ability to get it. We're giving them another way.

The program grew out of talks I had had with Villa, one of our main retailers in Philly. I was talking with Jason Lutz, who owned the company, and said, "You know, I want to try and figure out a way to use the connection that these young folks have with our brand and our product. How can we use that to motivate them?"

"You know what, that's a good thought," he said. "Let me think it over."

He took that to his team and they came back to us with the idea for the program. I loved it.

Gazing out on those West Philly High students that first day, I could feel their skepticism. They had heard it before. Promises, promises. Nothing materialized. No follow-through. But we piloted the program with three schools in Philly, first at West Philly, then Imhotep Institute Charter High School and Kensington High School for the Creative and Performing Arts.

It began to work, but for me it was only a start.

When we first started it out, the rewards were given for how many As they earned on their report cards. Then I started thinking that there are some kids who, no matter how hard they work, just are not going to achieve As. So, we started to recognize and reward improvements on grades as well as attendance. If a kid comes to school every day, then he's got a good shot at being successful. It helps to show up.

Critics showed up to say that maybe we shouldn't be paying these kids to do what they should be doing anyway.

I don't see it as paying them to get grades. I see it as motivating them. The motivation is the product and the shoes and all that, but also the message that they can make better lives for themselves. The way they're going to do that is through education. The other part of this is that, hopefully, we can make education and getting good grades and coming to school "cool." By showing them that if they do these things, then they will be the ones rocking the Js in school. They're the ones wearing the Jordan gear. You're the "cool guy" now. It's about how can we make it cool to be a good student.

That was one of the reasons that I fell off that path and

stopped focusing on school when I was young, because it wasn't cool. It wasn't cool to be the "teacher's pet," or to be the kid with the best grades and all that. That wasn't cool anymore. To be cool, I had to hang out in the streets and act crazy. I think that we can help to turn that perspective around to where it's cool to get As and good grades because the smart kids are now the ones that are laced with the gear.

If we can help provide that motivation, why not?

Our success with these first efforts in Philly motivated us to grow and expand our connections with students. In four cities—Philly, Chicago, Houston, and L.A.—we established community programs to invest in students from middle school through high school and into college, where the Jordan Brand Wings Scholars Program provides full-ride funding for dozens of students every year. And it continues to grow.

The idea for the funding began with H and my good friend and colleague Shauncey Mashia, Jordan Brand's global community brand manager. The three of us were trying to figure out a way to help worthy students pay for college. We began collaborating with the Rockefeller Philanthropy Advisors and the United Negro College Fund.

But it all started with the Little Black Pearl.

WHEN THE LITTLE Black Pearl students came out to Nike to work with our designers, one of the students sidled up to me when we were walking across the campus.

"Okay," he said, "let's say I get into business and want to wind up like you at a place like this. How do I make that happen?"

I wanted to respond: "Work your ass off and get lucky."

Instead, I said: "Go to school, keep learning, work hard—and build relationships. Make strong connections with people who can help you along the way."

"Like you?" he asked.

I laughed. We laughed. "Yep," I said.

Young people often talk to me about planning their careers, and I always give them this advice. I never thought about what my next job was going to be. My thing is this: If I give 100 percent to whatever it is that I'm currently doing, then what's next will materialize because I'm going to do a great job at what I'm doing now. If I'm busy thinking about what's next, then I'm not focused on doing what's now. I'm not giving all my effort to what I'm doing now. That's the way I approach it. I'm not thinking about a checklist for my career path. I'm going to give my all to what I'm doing today, and the next opportunity will show up. And it always has.

"Please tell me one specific piece of advice," he said.

We kept walking.

"Prepare well for job interviews," I said, "and answer the questions clearly. But also aim high. Tell the interviewers your goals, what you really hope to accomplish."

I thought back to graduating from Temple; I was in my thirties. To be able to start a career at that point in my life proves that it can be done. The only reason for me to write about any of this is for it to hopefully inspire someone. To say, hey, I'm proof that no matter how bad things are, no matter how low things seem to be—because it doesn't get much lower than walking the penitentiary yard—you can still create success.

But I couldn't tell that to the student. The secret wasn't out yet. I was still keeping it inside.

"Thanks, Mr. Miller," he said. "When's lunch?"

BY THE TIME Laila and I had completed our interviews for this book and started writing the manuscript, I was a changed man, again.

Through the process, I was becoming free of the secret's toxic effect on my psyche. By describing my dual personality—the gangster hiding within the businessman—I was becoming one. My suffering was coming to an end.

But the remorse over my killing another Black boy in West Philly when I was sixteen would never ease—nor should it. Owning up to the fact that I had taken a life might begin to free me, but only to a certain point. I will forever mourn his loss. Moving forward, I know true peace will come only by offering up opportunities to other kids in my old shoes for options beyond the streets and the violence that still leads to senseless bloodshed. Hope can come through providing opportunities for self-advancement, like the ones I took advantage of when I was at my lowest. I will always be bound to the reality that I had killed a boy who was just like me.

I've had to work very hard to confront my feelings of guilt from the crimes I've committed, the life I've taken, and the many lives my past deeds have affected. I've had to reconcile that with the added guilt I felt from achieving what I've been able to accomplish upon my release from prison. And however difficult it may have been for me, I'm well aware that it pales in comparison to the pain I have caused. Out of all the people that I know, and all the people that I've done dirt with and been in jail with, why was I the one who was able to do what I'm doing and get to this point? I used to feel unworthy. What has helped me to make peace with it is that I appreciate it, and I'm willing to share whatever it is that I have. I think that is part of the reason for my achievements. I never quit going up to Graterford to see Wazir and the other brothers. I still look out for the brothers as much as I can and help out whoever I can. I believe part of the reason I've been blessed to have whatever I have is due to my willingness and conscious effort to share whatever I have with the people I care about—and those who can gain motivation from my tale.

An old guy told me once that if your hand is closed up, then nothing can get out of it, but nothing can get into it, either. I've always remembered that advice.

By talking to Laila, I began losing the fear of people finding out about my past. I'm getting to a point where I just kind of feel like, okay, it is what it is. I almost think that for most people, when they find out, they'll be amazed. They'll be like, "For real?! Get the fuck outta here! You mean you went through all that, and you've been able to do all this?"

Or they won't. They will judge me for having lived a life of crime, for having served two sentences for violent crimes and keeping all that inside. Some might judge me for having been dishonest for so many decades. It might affect their ability to trust me. And they would be entitled to come to that conclusion. I'm okay with that. A small price to pay.

The more immediate question facing me was: Would I be able to tell my peers? How would I tell Phil Knight? I felt a deep obligation to alert Phil and a few others, like MJ, that the friend and business executive they'd known for decades was coming to full life in the pages of this book. And that that "full life" held secrets that might disturb, shock, and perhaps disappoint.

Phil was special to me. He had had my back at Nike when others doubted me. He had cleared the path for the growth of Jordan Brand in the midst of competing brands within Nike. He always took my call, included me at crucial moments, and looked out for me. I felt close to Phil, as my boss and as a friend. Perhaps that was why I had to tell him—and why I feared telling him.

I was in no hurry, and I avoided it as long as possible, until the manuscript was all but complete. In December 2020, I sent Phil a text.

"I have something very personal I would like to talk to you about," I wrote. "I would prefer if we could meet in person, but virtual would do."

The COVID-19 virus was still raging through the country, and the Nike campus was closed, so it was a long shot that Phil and I would meet face-to-face. I sent the text on a Friday, hoping to get on his schedule the following week.

"I don't want to wait," he responded immediately. "Let's make this happen Monday."

"Great," I thought. "I guess I have to do it."

Phil arranged a FaceTime call Monday afternoon. I was at home in Portland. I think Phil might have been out of town, perhaps at his home in Bend, Oregon.

"One P.M. work for you?" Phil texted me that morning.

Yeah, it worked, but I was working myself up into a sweat. I had been carrying the secret around for more than forty years.

The thought of exposing my past to anyone beyond my family was extremely troubling. Phil Knight would be the first. Would he see it as a negative? Would he consider it almost a betrayal and wonder why I had never told him the truth? Would he see it as bad for the brand?

About twenty minutes before the scheduled call, my phone rang. "Can we just talk now?" Phil asked. I sighed and thought, "Well, here we go."

After catching up for a few minutes, I started to come out with it.

"For many years my daughter Laila has been pushing me to write my story in a book," I said.

"Great idea," Phil said.

"But I had been avoiding it, in part because I have been keeping part of my life a secret," I said. "Starting at age twelve I had brushes with the law and have been in and out of prison." I proceeded to list all of my criminal convictions, my time behind bars, my relying on education release to turn my life around.

It took Phil a few seconds to take it all in. There was silence on the other end of the line. We looked at one another on-screen for what seemed like an eternity. Then he leaned in.

He said that he thought it was an amazing story and that I absolutely need to tell it.

He wanted to know if he could help. Did I have a cowriter, an agent, a publisher? Yes, to all three, I responded. I told him that the manuscript was almost complete.

He said it could be huge, and that he thought it was an inspirational story that could help a lot of people who need to hear it.

The call ended with Phil asking if he could read the manuscript and volunteering to help out in any way. When his face disappeared from the screen, I was relieved, at first. I took a few deep breaths. I had hoped Phil might react well, but this was beyond my expectations. Sitting alone, the fact that I had told Phil the secret began to sink in. And he had stood with me. I felt validated, and gratified.

WHEN I TOLD Michael Jordan about this book his reaction was supportive and encouraging. By the time I shared the secret with my peers, I had arrived at a place where I was ready to face any repercussions or consequences—positive or negative. I had been an integral part of taking Jordan Brand from a shoe company to a sustainable global athletic sportswear leader. I had helped lead the Portland Trail Blazers from a second-rate NBA team to a thriving NBA franchise. But no matter what I have acquired or what status I have achieved—none of that makes me who I am. If it all went away, I would be fine. I would find a way through.

The time had come in my life to take any and all risks to be free. If the definition of courage is that one has fear, confronts it, and does what he must anyway—then I was ready.

Besides, Laila and the rest of my family know the whole man and love me anyway. And that's good enough for me.

EPILOGUE

Back to Prison

*T*he prison system in the United States is a business. It's always been a business, and it's an even bigger business now than when I was inside. The money that's spent on warehousing people is money that could be invested in a more humane and productive way, and that could have a much more positive impact on people's lives and, I feel, on society as a whole. When I served time, Pennsylvania prisons had work-release programs, education-release programs, halfway houses, and more, with the established goal of reforming and releasing those who had been found guilty of committing a crime. Participation in these programs was incentivized with early release. Those programs have been greatly diminished, if not dissolved altogether.

When I was incarcerated, Villanova, Montgomery County Community College, Temple, and Cheyney State University were all bringing classes into Graterford.

"Now there might be a couple classes offered," Wazir tells me, "but the inmates hardly take advantage of it because there is no incentive."

When I was there, a person could take classes with a goal in mind. The classes led to the program, and the program led to an earlier release—either to work for a guaranteed job or to further pursue an education. Most of those options are not available anymore, so the incentive is not the same for incarcerated people today.

I've said that my decision to begin taking classes was in no way motivated by any higher aspirations for a new life. I was looking for the fastest way to get myself out of prison. I viewed the education-release programs at Graterford as a means to an end, at first. But the more I took advantage of the opportunities Graterford offered, the clearer the picture of a different kind of life became. The courses I took in those days were paid for using Federal Pell Grant subsidies and other student loans as well as state funding. Without those classes inside Graterford being subsidized I never would have been able to get started.

Time was on my side in this respect, since the Violent Crime Control and Law Enforcement Act of 1994 ended prisoners' access to Pell Grants. This major funding cut ended an era of prison educational opportunities. The second chance that I was given would no longer be available.

Malcolm X's experiences at Norfolk Prison Colony in Massachusetts in the 1940s, with its extensive library and culture of rehabilitation through education, were pivotal to his development. He described in his autobiography how being in that environment, with its links to institutions such as Harvard, Emerson, and Boston College, "represented the most enlightened form of prison that I have ever heard of. In place of the atmosphere of malicious gossip, perversion, grafting, hateful guards, there was more relative 'culture,' as 'culture' is interpreted in prisons. A high percentage of the Norfolk Prison Colony inmates went in for 'intellectual' things, group discussions, debates, and such."[*]

Today, there are minimal prospects for prisoner education scattered about the country. There are a few state-run and privately funded programs such as the California Promise Grant; Cornell Prison Education Program; Hudson Link for Higher Education in Prisons; Villanova's inmate education program, which became underwritten by the school itself after loss of the Pell Grant funds; and the Inside-Out Prison Exchange Program founded at my alma mater, Temple University.

The only program I know of resembling what the state of Pennsylvania did for us is the Indiana Department of Corrections Education Incentive System, where prisoners earn credit toward early release or "Time-Cut" for completing educational programs like a G.E.D., an A.A., and a B.A.

The Bard Prison Initiative in New York State has awarded more than five hundred associate and bachelor's degrees to incarcerated people at six institutions since its founding in 1999. The program has a 4 percent recidivism rate, compared to the national average of around 60 percent. And I know that many colleges and universities across the nation have created programs to bring professors into prisons or those incarcerated onto campus.

------

[*] Malcolm X and Alex Haley, *The Autobiography of Malcolm X* (New York: Ballantine Books, 1992), p. 182.

"Knowledge makes a man unfit to be a slave," said the scholar, acclaimed orator, and formerly enslaved Frederick Douglass.

The truth in that statement is self-evident. Allowing incarcerated people access to education liberates them and helps to make our society safer overall. This statement has been studied and verified by many, including the RAND Corporation's comprehensive analysis "Evaluating the Effectiveness of Correctional Education" published in 2013. The findings were no surprise to me:

- Correctional education improves inmates' chances of not returning to prison.

- Inmates who participate in correctional education programs had 43 percent lower odds of recidivating than those who did not. This translates to a reduction of 13 percentage points in the risk of recidivating.

- It may improve their chances of obtaining employment after release. The odds of obtaining employment post release among inmates who participated in correctional education were 13 percent higher than the odds for those who did not participate in correctional education.

- Inmates exposed to computer-assisted instruction learned slightly more in reading and substantially more in math in the same amount of instructional time.

- Providing correctional education can be cost-effective when it comes to reducing recidivism.

According to the Bureau of Justice Statistics, the amount of taxpayer dollars spent incarcerating prisoners dwarfs the amount spent to educate them. Taxpayers currently spend $80 million keeping 2.3 million people in prison, on average $32,000 per inmate annually, and those numbers have risen consistently over the years since I've been out.[*]

Nevertheless, two thirds of prisoners have no access to higher education, and access to even the basic building blocks—books— has increasingly come under attack.

My mission, therefore, is to inform and influence public opinion about how crucial access to education has been in making my story possible. Congress finally lifting the ban on Pell Grants for incarcerated people, which is scheduled to take effect by mid-2023, will be vital to improving accessibility to educational opportunities. Combined with incentivized, high-quality education and work-release options for incarcerated people, I see this as a primary key to prison reform. I want to show just how life-changing incentivized inmate education was for me. Had I just been warehoused at Graterford, forced into inmate labor, and offered no opportunity for self-improvement, I might still be sitting there, or worse. I aim to lend my voice to establishing a reformative and rehabilitative emphasis to the prison system, in addition to sentencing reforms and removing the overall stigma attached to people who've been incarcerated that often hinders their ability to achieve.

The time has come for me to devote myself to shining a light

---

[*] https://www.themarshallproject.org/2019/12/17/the-hidden-cost
-of-incarceration

on the proven value of rehabilitation in the prison system; to advocating for reviving education-release programs, trade school programs, and work-release programs; to improving access to books and learning materials; to banning the box; and to helping give both currently and formerly incarcerated people the opportunity to succeed. Consider this my new purpose.

ACKNOWLEDGMENTS

LARRY MILLER

I have been Blessed to live an amazing journey and there have been so many people that have been there with love and support along the way. Even when I didn't deserve that love and support based on the life I was living. It starts with my family. My mother and father, sisters, brothers, aunts and uncles, cousins, nieces and nephews, and of course my beautiful children and grandchildren. But it also includes many people that I have met and connected with over the years. Many that I consider family because of the love and support we give each other. It's way too long of a list to name and I know I would miss someone if I tried.

That being said, there is one person that I must thank for making this book possible and that is my daughter, Laila. Without her persistence and inspiration, it would not have happened. She also has done an incredible amount of hard work as we have gone through this process. She was patient with me as I wrestled

ACKNOWLEDGMENTS

with sharing the story I had kept secret for so long. She pushed me when needed and gave me the time and space when needed. I want to say thank you, La.

Thank you for giving me the courage and confidence to share this story that I hope can positively affect some lives. Thank you for allowing me to unload this burden of carrying this secret around for forty years. Thank you for ending the nightmares and migraines that this secret was causing. If it wasn't for you, I'd still be carrying this secret around with the fear that I would be exposed. You made me realize it is time to kill this secret and share my story so it may inspire others.

Thank you, La.

LAILA LACY

First, I want to thank you, Dad, for allowing me the honor of telling your story with you. It's been so inspirational and healing for me, and I'm forever grateful.

Thanks to my mother, Pearl Jackson, and to Ethel Jackson, Benjamin Jackson, Lucille Bowen, and Vernon Bowen, for your love, for raising me, and for being so instrumental in keeping our family together. Many thanks to my sisters, Aleah Rice, Raquel Jennings, and Angela Jennings. Thank you, aunties Eileen Miller, Gloria Evans, Florence Guillory, Theresa Turner, Sandra Daye, Theresa Harrington, Benita Baker, and so many others who've shown me the way. Shouts out to all my cousins for your love, laughter, and support.

Thank you, Kai Flowers, for being my trusted sister/friend

since first grade, and the entire Flowers family for always treating me like one of your own. Thank you, Jennifer Foster, for being such a beautiful spirit, and for always offering me a safe place to land whenever I come back home. Thank you to my Howard University family for your guidance and grounding.

Thank you, West Philly. You will always be home.

BOTH

Thanks so much to Jeff Freid for your guidance, and Harry Jaffe for your contributions and insight. We could not have done this without either of you. Thank you, David Larabell and CAA, Mauro DiPreta and William Morrow & Company, and David Black for understanding our vision and aspiration, and helping us make this a reality.

We are thankful for the entire Miller family, the Jackson family, and all who have had a hand in this book's completion. If we've forgotten anybody, please charge it to our heads and not our hearts.

ABOUT THE AUTHORS

LARRY MILLER was appointed the first chairman of the Jordan Brand Advisory Board in January 2019. Prior to that he was president of Jordan Brand from 1999 to 2006, and from 2012 to 2018. In that role he was responsible for all aspects of the iconic athletic apparel firm, from supply chains and advertising to marketing and growing the global brand. Under his leadership, Jordan Brand has grown from a $150 million basketball shoe company to a $4 billion athletic footwear and apparel brand. Miller helped found the Jordan Brand at Nike in 1999 before becoming president of the Portland Trail Blazers from 2007 to 2012, after which he returned to Jordan Brand. Miller graduated with honors from Temple University in 1982 and earned an MBA from La Salle University. He has served on the board of directors of Self Enhancement, Inc., and the Oregon Business Council. A passionate advocate for education and mentorship, he's taken leadership roles with the Urban League and Junior Achievement.

LAILA LACY, a native of Philadelphia, graduated from Central High School. She earned a degree from Howard University in Washington, D.C., where she studied psychology and human communications and has studied at New York's Bank Street Graduate School of Education. Lacy taught middle school for the New York Board of Education and later served as a business development manager for several mortgage banking firms in California. In addition to collaborating on her father's memoir, she's been a tutor, writing coach, and school volunteer, and she's written op-eds and product reviews that have been featured in several online magazines. She lives in Southern California with her husband and three children.